Italian Riviera

Italian Riviera – A Classic Coastline

Opposite: on the beach at Alassio

The Italian Riviera: the name conjures up images of palm trees and cacti, thick *macchia* and vast fields of cloves, elegant hotels and suntanned millionaires. The Riviera certainly is all that – a lush and fragrant sunny region between the mountains and the sea. But the three million or so visitors who come here each year are attracted not only by its endless fields of flowers and its beautiful coastline, but also by its thousands of years of history and its cultural legacy. The explorer Christopher Columbus and the violinist Nicolò Paganini are just two of the many great names to have been associated with the region's capital, Genoa.

Apricale clings to the hillside

Genoa has been unjustly neglected for some time now. It was much praised by travellers of previous centuries, especially Gustave Flaubert who in 1845 referred to it enthusiastically as 'a city built entirely of marble, with gardens full of roses, and a beauty which tears at the soul'. Bordighera and San Remo are rather like elderly ladies accustomed to better times, but both have adapted to the exigencies of modern tourism; Portofino does its best to shield its VIPs from over-curious eyes; Alassio revolves entirely around entertainment; Albenga exudes a medieval atmosphere; and the ever popular villages that make up the Cinque Terre have accepted a moderate amount of tourism in order to save their dizzyingly steep vineyard terraces from destruction by roads and motorways.

Religious motif in Genoa

5

The Ligurian Mediterranean coast also has a less attractive side, however. Alongside the breathtaking *bellezza* there are also the problems faced by Genoa's Old Town, the traffic-choked Via Aurelia, and the faceless concrete high rise apartment blocks surrounding many of the resorts. These scars have largely been hidden by the Riviera's ever fascinating natural scenery, its perfectly organised beach resorts and its picturesque mountain villages. So far, anyway.

Liguria has two faces: the resorts along the coast which extend like a string of pearls from Bordighera in the west to the Cinque Terre in the east, and the region inland. The area which has been marketed as the Italian Riviera for the past 150 years comprises not only the highly-regarded coastal resorts, such as San Remo and Portofino, with their thousands of sunbathers, but also the peaceful mountain villages further inland, often only a few miles away from the sea, where time seems to have stood still.

Gathering the crop

Liguria is relatively small – a narrow strip of land squeezed in between the mountains and the sea. The luxuriant Mediterranean vegetation along the coast contrasts vividly with the stark and severe mountain scenery higher up, and the Ligurians down on the coast who have lived off seafaring and fishing for centuries seem to have very

The coastline is mostly rocky

Vernazza – one of the Cinque Terre

little in common with their compatriots higher up in the mountains, who grow produce as best they can on the often barren soil.

Position and size

Liguria covers a total surface area of just 5,418sq km (2,090sq miles), which makes it the third-smallest region in Italy after the Molise and the Val d'Aosta. It ranges from 7.5km (4½ miles) to 38km (23 miles) in width, and is roughly 275km (170 miles) long, extending around the Gulf of Genoa, the northernmost part of the Ligurian Sea. The mountains and hills form the *Regione Liguria*, accurately described in the tourist brochures as a colourful mix of the Alps and the Apennines; the point where the two mighty mountain ranges meet is generally considered to be the 465-m (1,525-ft) high Cole di Cadibona near Savona. The highest peak in Liguria is Monte Saccarello (2,200m/7,217ft) in the Western Alps, on the Franco-Italian border. The narrow coastal strip connects with a series of mountain valleys, most of them quite short.

Within the space of just a few miles they rise steeply from the Mediterranean climatic zone, with its palm trees, olive groves and vineyards, into the Alpine zone full of beech, larch and pine, creating the sharp contrast in landscape for which Liguria is so well-known. The proximity of the mountains to the coast creates climatic extremes: the Mediterranean southern slopes are right next to the kind of scenery more often associated with Central or Northern Europe.

The streams that pour down the mountainsides and through the valleys can often burst their banks and become raging torrents; this has happened increasingly often recently, and many rivers and streams are now bordered by concrete walls to allow the water to crash down into the valleys unhindered. Many of the mountain slopes which used to absorb much of the water have now been built on and concreted over, resulting in disastrous flooding of streets and cellars – not only in Genoa itself but many other coastal resorts as well. Landslides are also a common problem in Liguria; anyone driving inland after a period of heavy rain should check with the authorities beforehand to see which mountain routes are still passable.

Liguria's fragile geological equilibrium can be traced to the fact that the region is composed primarily of soft sandstone and marl, formed during the Cretaceous Period (65–130 million years ago) and extending across the whole of western Liguria as well as a large area to the east of Genoa. The Apennine peaks behind Genoa and Savona consist of various kinds of serpentine stone – including green serpentine, without which the fascinating light-and-dark effect of many Ligurian churches and palazzi would be unthinkable. One classic serpentine mountain is Monte Beigua (*see Route 5, page 47*). Also fascinating geologically is the limestone region, formed between 200 and 250 million years ago, which characterises the mountain landscape between Albenga and Savona; it is a paradise for climbers and potholers. Inland from Finale Ligure and also near Toirano and Ventimiglia, several limestone caverns formerly inhabited by the earliest Ligurians are now open to tourists.

Apart from serpentine and marble (famous examples include *portoro* from Portofino, the red-and-green marble from Levanto and green marble from Pegli), slate has long been a popular construction material in Liguria. There are still slate quarries today in the Valle Fontanabuona near Lavagna, and many of the houses in Ligurian villages still have delightful slate portals.

Quarrying for slate in the Valle Fontanabuona

Climate and when to go

It was the mild and temperate climate which attracted (predominantly English) tourists to the Italian Riviera in the middle of the 19th century. Unlike today's visitors who occupy the Ligurian beaches from late spring to early autumn, they came to spend the winter here; unsurprisingly, in view of the mild climate. The average winter temperatures along the coast seldom sink below 8°C (46°F), and are as high as 10°C (50°F) between Alassio and San Remo – something only experienced again down at the Gulf of Naples. The summer temperatures are also very bearable thanks to a fresh sea breeze, averaging between 22°C (71°C) and 24°C (75°C). Snow falls in Genoa on an average of two days a year, and two to six days in La Spezia. The months with the lowest rainfall are July and August.

High season at the coast

7

Liguria is a great place to visit all year round. Sunbathing and swimming fans will doubtless opt for the summer months; fans of culture and history tend to visit the region in spring and autumn, when the roads are less full and the hotels and campsites have space again. Or why not visit in winter – just like the English did one hundred and fifty years ago?

Nature and the environment

Liguria has 13 nature reserves: 10 regional parks *(Parchi naturali regionali)* and three regional reserves *(Riserve naturali regionali)*. Among the finest of the latter is the Isola Gallinara, an 11-hectare (27-acre) island in the province of Savona. Only a few miles away from the hopelessly over-built-up coast, it shows what the flora in the region looked like before the advent of tourism (the island can only be visited by prior arrangement with the owners).

Monte di Portofino

The Rio Torsero nature reserve (4 hectares/9 acres), also located in the province of Savona, is famous for its astonishingly well-preserved fossils from the Pliocene Era (5.2–1.3 million years ago).

Inland from Chiavari in the province of Genoa, the Aveto nature reserve (10,380 hectares/25,600 acres) contains several lakes dating from the Ice Age and rich flora typical of marshland areas.

The Monte di Portofino nature reserve (4,650 hectares/ 11,500 acres) in Santa Maria Lighure is a real highlight of any trip to Liguria, with its scenic beauty and cultural sights such as the monastery of San Fruttuoso *(see Route 2, page 31)* – and the same goes for the five famous villages that make up the Cinque Terre *(see Route 3, page 36)*, which are protected by the nature reserve that also includes Montemarcello.

Liguria shows its colours

The 317-km (196-mile) long Riviera coast is a sight in itself; mostly rocky, it has preserved its original character in only a few areas. However, swimming fans can rest assured that in recent years only around 3 percent of the Ligurian beaches have been off-limits (Tuscany and the Northern Adriatic were the only places to score better), though it should be borne in mind that towns along the Western Riviera *(Riviera di Ponente*, provinces of Savona and Imperia) outdid their Eastern Riviera *(Riviera di Levante)* counterparts such as Genoa and La Spezia, whose harbours cause quite a bit of pollution.

Liguria has more forests than any other part of Italy: they cover 53 percent of its surface. Since much of the woodland faces south, forest fires are quite common.

Population

Liguria has a population of roughly 1.7 million. The population density is far above Italy's average, even though

the number of inhabitants has been gradually decreasing over the past few years. Most of the population lives along the narrow coastal strip. New job opportunities in industry, and especially in tourism, are leading to a gradual depopulation of the remote mountain regions. The empty houses and often completely deserted villages are providing welcome accommodation for Northern and Central Europeans weary of civilisation, and also Italians from neighbouring regions who have found a second home in Liguria, either for a few months each year or permanently.

The elderly stay on

Language

Even Italian speakers can be forgiven for not understanding much of what is spoken along the Riviera. Ligurian is one of the Northern Italian dialects, and is really hard to understand even for other Italians. Its distinctive features include a tendency to contract various sounds, miss out consonants between vowels and alter the sound of long 'o' s and 'a's. For instance, *nuovo* (new) becomes *növu*, *nuora* (daughter-in-law) becomes *nöa*, and *cuore* (heart) is contracted down to *cö*. Place names tend to be noticeably different from the official ones: Genoa is known to the locals as *Sena*, Savona as *Sana*, Rovereto as *Ruveóu*, and Arenzano as *Aensén*. The list could be continued indefinitely – all the way to San Remo, which was originally known as *San Romolo* and then changed into the local dialect version *San Römu*, before finally being 'translated' into written Italian as San Remo.

Economy

In terms of per capita income, Liguria is the third-wealthiest Italian region after the Val d'Aosta and Lombardy. Tourism is doubtless one of the main reasons for this relative prosperity: the Riviera is the most popular region

Albisola Marina ceramics

The port of La Spezia

Vineyards at Corniglia

of Italy for the tourist trade. Here again the double face of Liguria becomes apparent: 80 percent of tourism is along the coast, and just 20 percent further inland.

Iron, steel, machinery and shipbuilding are cornerstones of local industry, as is olive oil production. The Ligurian harbours turn over a record amount of goods. Genoa is the most important harbour in the country, and as a passenger port only third in importance to Brindisi and Venice. Along with La Spezia and Savona (Italy's export harbour for Fiat and Lancia cars), Genoa handles one fifth of Italian passenger traffic and one sixth of its goods traffic.

Along the Western Riviera, flower cultivation is a very important industry, and the innumerable greenhouses are a distinctive feature of the landscape. Although only a small proportion of the wine produced in the region is exported, viticulture is also a factor in the local economy, with three Ligurian wines having a DOC, the government mark of quality.

As far as arts and crafts are concerned, there are ceramics from Albisola, bells from Avegno, filigree jewellery from Campo Ligure, chairs from Chiavari, velvet from Zoagli, brocade and damask from Lorsica, bobbin lace from Portofino, Santa Margherita Ligure, Paraggi and Camogli, glass from Altare, church clocks from Recco, Uscio and Pietra Ligure, toys from the Valle Fontanabuona, and lavender from Pietrabruna.

Politics and Administration

Liguria, officially the *Regione Liguria*, is one of Italy's twenty regions. Its capital is Genoa (Italian *Genova,* pop. 660,000), and Liguria is divided up into the four provinces of Genoa, Imperia, La Spezia and Savona.

Politically the Italian regions are anything but federal; their statutes allow for no independent decision-making. Though the system is far from feudal, most of the regions are still very much under the control of the central government in Rome.

The Alta Via

The very well-marked hiking route known as the *Alta Via dei Monti Liguri* begins at the coast close to Ventimiglia, runs the length of the Ligurian Apennines, and ends around 440km (270 miles) further on at Ceparana, north of La Spezia. The longest hiking route on Italian soil, it is divided into 44 different sections, each between 5km (3 miles) and 17km (10 miles) long, and covers differences in elevation of up to 952m (3,100ft). The highest point of the Alta Via is the summit of Monte Saccaretto (2,200m/7,200ft) on the Franco-Italian border.

What makes this Ligurian hiking route so special is the sheer wealth of natural scenery along the way, the fascinating difference between the Mediterranean landscape on one side and the Alpine one on the other, and also the fact that many sections of it follow ancient medieval trading routes. It therefore leads through remote Ligurian mountain villages that are gradually being depopulated, and past the imposing ruins of several old fortified sites that were so essential in this strategically disputed region. Don't worry about not being fit enough, or good enough at trekking: there are villages dotted every few miles along the route.

A wealth of scenery

Andrea Doria – Liguria's Local Hero

In Italian history books Andrea Doria is praised as the hero who saved Liguria. In reality, the legendary figure was a clever and capricious mercenary leader, who made a series of skilful political moves in order to become the ruler of Genoa for thirty years.

Andrea Doria was born in 1466 in Oneglia, and after the deaths of his parents he embarked on a military career in the service of all kinds of different lords, including Pope Innocent VIII, the Neapolitan kings Ferdinand I and Alphonse II, and the Borgias' rival Giovanni della Rovere. He fought against an uprising on Corsica, was universally feared by pirates, ran a used-ship business, defeated the papal-imperial fleet that tried to conquer Genoa, and then placed his vessels at the service of the French king François I. Together with his cousin Filippino he defeated the fleet of Emperor Charles V, then suddenly changed sides and entered the Emperor's service only a few weeks later. With the support of Charles V he became the ruler of Genoa, controlling the city's fortunes for the next 30 years until his death in 1569.

Historical Highlights

Palaeolithic Period Traces of human habitation in various Ligurian caves, some up to 300,000 years old.

Bronze Age Tens of thousands of cave paintings appear in the Vallée des Merveilles.

6th century BC The Ligurians are driven out of the Po Plain by invading Gauls. Some of them settle today's Liguria, mixing with the local tribes and becoming fishermen and coastal traders.

5th century BC By this time, Genoa has developed into a sizable metropolis, enjoying commercial links with the Greeks and Etruscans.

3rd century BC Rome launches her policy of expansionism, and soon realises the strategic advantage of Genoa and its rivieras.

180BC Roman conquest of Liguria. Under Roman rule the region experiences a long period of economic and cultural prosperity. Genoa and a number of other Ligurian harbours become Roman naval bases.

5th–6th centuries Confusion reigns after the fall of the Roman Empire. The region is occupied by the Goths for a time before being ruled by Byzantium. Despite the upheavals, Genoa and smaller ports such as La Spezia and Savona continue to develop as trading ports.

641 Genoa is conquered by King Rothan of Lombardy.

9th–10th centuries The Ligurian coastal towns are subjected to repeated attacks by Saracens and Norman pirates. Genoa is destroyed by the Saracens in 936. Around the middle of the 10th century Liguria is divided up into three marches by the Italian king, Berengar III.

11th–12th centuries Under the leadership of the pope, the Genoese ally themselves with Pisa and launch a series of military campaigns against the Saracen-held islands of Corsica and Sardinia. After defeating the Saracens in 1148, Genoa begins to assert itself as the dominant power in the Mediterranean. The Crusades and trade with the Orient bring untold prosperity to the region. Genoese ships carry cargoes from the eastern Mediterranean, through the straits of Gibraltar to northern Europe. As the old feudal structure weakens, the main towns in the region all assert their independence.

1284 Genoa defeats its arch rival Pisa in the naval battle of Meloria, off Livorno, clearing the way for supremacy as a maritime power, although it still has to compete strongly with Venice. By the end of the 13th century, Genoa has possessions and trading posts as far afield as Constantinople, the Black Sea, Armenia and Syria; the population of the city has swelled to more than 100,000, making it one of the largest cities in Europe.

14th century Genoa is racked by serious internal power struggles between the various patrician families supporting the pope (Guelphs) and those supporting the Holy Roman Emperor (Ghibellines). Despite this, the feuding families succeed in amassing vast fortunes, and proceed to construct their magnificent palaces not only in Genoa but all along the rivieras to the east and west. There are constant rebellions by other towns against Genoese hegemony in the region. Bitter economic rivalry leads to increased fragmentation, and there is a return to feudalism. Local nobles create their own fiefdoms protected by hilltop castles along the coast. Towns are heavily fortified.

1339 After a series of invasions by the French and others, Simon Boccanegra is elected the first doge of Genoa.

1346–8 Liguria is ravaged by a severe epidemic of the Black Death.

1378–81 Genoa is soundly defeated by Venice in the Chioggia War, signalling the end of its maritime supremacy. In subsequent decades it becomes the plaything of foreign powers, including the Viscontis and the Sforzas from Milan and France.

Early 15th century Genoese merchants create the Banco di San Giorgio, which provides a solid foundation for the ultimate development of the city into a world financial centre.

1451 Birth of Christopher Columbus, Genoa's most famous son.

1522 Genoa is brutally sacked by the Spanish army.

1528 Andrea Doria, Genoa's most beloved local hero (*see page 11*), liberates Genoa from French dominion and rules the city single-handed for 30 years.

mid-16th century onwards Its bankers having gained control of most of the international monetary network, Genoa is the world's leading financial city. The Spanish kings raise money here for their campaigns, and the wealth of the New World is funnelled through Genoa before being distributed elsewhere.

1576 Genoa receives a republican constitution.

1608 Genoa assumes the status of free port.

17th century The Genoese position at the head of international banking is gradually usurped by the new major European power, namely Portugal.

1684 The French under Louis XIV bombard and enter Genoa without encountering resistance.

1746 Liguria is occupied by the Austrians, who, in alliance with Spain, impose a cruelly oppressive regime. But the Austrians are driven out by popular resistance and Genoa keeps its independence until 1796.

1796 The aristocratic Genoese Republic is conquered by French revolutionary troops under Napoleon Bonaparte and transformed into the French-controlled 'Ligurian Republic'.

1805 The Ligurian Republic becomes a part of France, and the French attempt to introduce revolutionary concepts into the feudal domains.

1815 After the downfall of Napoleon, a new European order is imposed at the Congress of Vienna. Liguria is made over to the Kingdom of Piedmont-Sardinia as the 'Duchy of Genoa'.

After 1815 Genoa is a centre of political activism in the Italian freedom struggle.

1821–34 Three anti-Piedmontese uprisings by the Ligurians are crushed.

1849–59 Ligurian freedom-fighters Giuseppe Mazzini, Giuseppe Garibaldi, Goffredo Mameli and Nino Bixio lead the Risorgimento (movement for Italian independence).

1860 Garibaldi sets sail on his expedition to overthrow the bourbon dynasty ruling Sicily and southern Italy. Nice and the region surrounding it are ceded to France.

1861 Liguria becomes part of the new Kingdom of Italy under Vittorio Emanuele II. Genoa develops a key role as commercial and industrial centre.

1887 On 23 February an earthquake causes serious damage to parts of Western Liguria.

1915 Italy enters World War I on the side of Britain and France, holding the front in the Dolomites.

1922 onwards Genoa becomes a major centre of resistance to Mussolini and the forces of fascism that have enveloped the country. The movement becomes more hostile after Italy enters World War II on the side of Germany in 1940.

1943 The resistance movement manages to rescue Genoa's shipyards and other industrial installations from destruction by the German army.

1945 In April, the resistance launches a successful uprising in advance of the country's liberation by the Allies.

1947 On 10 February the central and upper parts of the Roia Valley as far as the Colle di Tenda are ceded to France, under the terms of the Treaty of Paris.

1945 onwards Badly damaged during the war, Genoa is rebuilt and emerges as Italy's leading seaport, making a significant contribution to the nation's postwar economic prosperity. New prosperity along the Riviera comes with the development of tourism.

1992 onwards The Riviera coast and regions inland suffer serious and recurrent flooding.

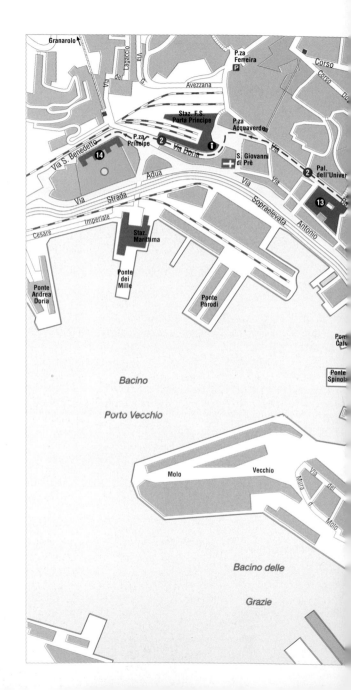

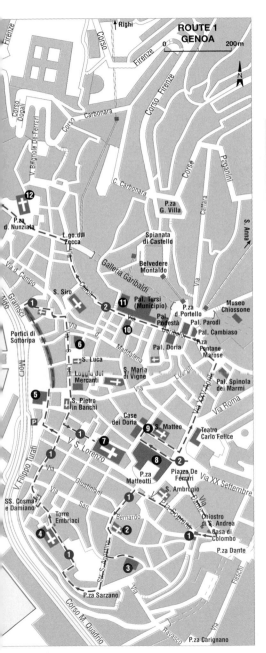

ROUTE 1
GENOA
0 — 200m

Genoa harbour

San Lorenzo Cathedral

Palazzo Reale

Route 1

★★ Genoa

Genoa is not an 'easy' city from the tourist point of view. Instead of displaying its treasures proudly, it hides them away behind dark palazzo facades and traffic-ridden streets. The Genoese have always jealously guarded their privacy, and rather than attract tourists they have largely preferred to divert them away to the Riviera resorts. Recently however, the city has received a facelift, and the light-grey jumble of houses jammed between the mountains and the sea now sports the odd yellow, red or brown restored palazzo, often with a beautiful garden attached.

History

The harbour today

The Ligurians who lived here before the Romans arrived traded from this natural harbour with Greeks, Etruscans, Phoenicians and Celts – and the Romans themselves, to whom Genoa lent its heartfelt support during the Punic Wars, knew just how strategically important the town was. After periods of Ostrogoth, Byzantine, Lombard and Frankish rule, Genoa began to get more self-confident. It defied the dreaded Saracens, and dared confront the pirates on the high seas. The Genoese merchants and mariners seemed to like the sea: they took part in the Crusades, founded trading posts in the Orient and brought back large amounts of booty, including the mortal relics of John the Baptist, back to their homeland. Rivalry with Pisa came to a head with the latter's defeat at sea in 1284, at the Battle of Meloria off Livorno, and Genoa also beat the Venetians (initially at least) in a battle fought close to the Dalmatian island of Curzola. Genoa had possessions and trading posts in Constantinople, the Black Sea, Armenia and Syria; it owned Corsica and part of Sardinia; it had harbours and storage depots in North Africa. By 1300 it was one of the world's major powers.

18

A historic port of call
Recalling the days of sail

However, instead of enjoying their newfound wealth in peace, the city's principal families began to argue among themselves: the Fieschi, Grimaldi, Guarchi and Montalto fought against the Doria, Spinola, Adorno and Fregoso. Genoa was threatened by the Aragonese, and subsequently conquered by Venice; it was then forced to submit to the patronage of several different lords. When America was discovered, Genoa lost its importance as a maritime power and was very nearly defeated during battles between France and Spain. At this stage, however, Andrea Doria (*see page 11*) arrived on the scene. A skilful, experienced admiral, he turned his back on his lord, King François I of France, and offered France's arch-enemy, Emperor Charles V, money and ships. In 1528 Genoa became an independent republic, and until the 1560s Andrea Doria was its undisputed ruler.

Even though Genoa had suffered much political damage on the world stage, it became prosperous in the 16th and 17th centuries. New churches were built, as were magnificent palaces, all of them very much in the style of the Palazzo Doria, built by its namesake. Impressive avenues were also built, and their splendour astonished all the Europeans who visited the city. Then Genoa was once again exposed to various warring states: Savoy, France, Austria, the French again during the Napoleonic era, Britain, Austria, France yet again – until the Genoese republic was made part of Piedmont at the Congress of Vienna in 1815, and eventually part of the new united Italy in 1860.

Today, Genoa is still the most important harbour in Italy. Nevertheless, the Columbus Year of 1992, upon which the locals had placed so many hopes, failed to live up to them; the city did not receive the expected boost to its fortunes. These days Genoa is usually mentioned in the papers for the problems it is having with its Old Town rather than for any of its many artistic and architectural masterpieces, which remain under-appreciated even by many Italians themselves.

Local passions

19

Tour 1 - the Old Town

Genoa has a very large Old Town, covering 4sq km (1½sq miles), and considered to be the largest in Europe. Unfortunately it has not been looked after properly. Around half of its 40,000 inhabitants are from other countries: while the Italians are gradually abandoning the *carrugi* (small dark alleyways) and the uncomfortable apartments, immigrants from Northern and Central Africa are moving – many of them illegally – into the empty houses and using them as provisional accommodation. This Old Town is the heart of Genoa, however, and has been ever since the city's *castello* hill was first populated in the 6th century BC by Ligurian settlers.

From the modern **Piazza De Ferrari**, the square with the most traffic in Genoa, head for the **Piazza Dante**, where the past and the present both meet: two skyscrapers built in 1940 stand opposite the so-called Casa de Cristoforo Colombo, where the great explorer is supposed to have spent his childhood (the house is an 18th-century reconstruction). The adjacent 12th-century Romanesque cloister of Sant'Andrea has some impressive capitals, and beyond it is the **Porta Soprana** ❶, part of the former medieval fortifications.

On the way to the church of **San Donato** ❷ it's worth strolling through the streets of the Old Town, where crafts-

Piazza De Ferrari
Porta Soprana

Santa Maria di Castello

men can still be observed at work (e.g. in the Via Giustiniani); as you do so you'll realise just how much redevelopment is needed in this whole area. The church of San Donato represents one well-meant but utterly disastrous attempt at restoration (1888): the architect responsible, Alfredo d'Andrade, robbed the building almost entirely of its Romanesque character. Dominated by an octagonal Romanesque belfry, the three-aisled interior contains several Roman columns. Several noteworthy works of art inside the church include a late 14th-century *Madonna and Child* by Nicolò da Voltri, and an *Adoration of the Magi* by the Dutch painter Joos van Cleve, who lived in Genoa from 1526 to 1528.

One very good example of how successfully a cloister can be transformed into a museum is the **Museo de Architettura e Scultura Ligure ❸** (Tuesday to Saturday 9am–7.30pm, Sunday 9am–12.30pm), next to the Gothic church of Sant'Agostino. The exhibits provide a good general impression of Ligurian sculpture from the 6th to the 18th centuries. Highlights among these various architectural fragments, statues, frescoes and tomb slabs taken from Genoese churches include the *Tomb of Simon Boccanegra*, the first doge of Genoa, by a 16th-century Pisan artist, and the *Tomb of Margherita di Brabante* (completed in 1313 by Giovanni Pisano); she was the wife of Emperor Henry VII, and died of the plague in Genoa in 1311. The church of Sant'Agostino also serves a different purpose these days: it has been turned into a modern auditorium.

Perhaps the oldest of Genoa's 20 or so churches consecrated to the Virgin Mary is the Early Christian ★ **Santa Maria di Castello ❹**, now a largely Romanesque structure. It was built by the so-called *Magistri Antelami* from Northern Lombardy, who were also employed in the construction of new harbour installations. The Dominican monks who own the building today had a monastery with three cloisters attached to the three-aisled church during the 15th and early 16th century. Behind the modest facade there are gardens, frescoed walkways and broad loggias with fine views of the harbour. A small museum (daily 9am–noon and 3.30–6pm) also contains valuable liturgical manuscripts and incunabula.

Towering beside Santa Maria di Castello is the 12th-century **Torre Embriaci**, the best-preserved of the 66 or so privately owned towers of 13th-century Genoa. Even though other towers in the city had to remain under a height limit of 24m (78ft), the Torre Embriaci was allowed to retain its 41m (134ft) because of services rendered to the city by the Embriaci family during the Crusades.

Go along the Via Canneto il Curto (taking a detour via the Via Canneto il Lungo with its reliefs, friezes and slate and marble portals on the noble palazzi) as far as the

★ **Palazzo San Giorgio** ❺, one of the city's major landmarks. Built as a seat of government in 1260 by Guglielmo Boccanegra, the Genoese governor at that time, it served later as a town hall and a customs house. In the 15th century the influential Banco di San Giorgio made the building its headquarters. Genoa's banks were extremely powerful during the Renaissance period: they financed the wars and caprices of the Spanish Habsburg monarchy, when Charles V and Philip II controlled half the Mediterranean. On the first floor of the building, the medieval council chamber, assembly hall and the hall of the Capitano del Popolo are still open to the public. During recent restoration work on the outer walls of the palazzo, a bright and colourful façade fresco by Lazzaro Tavone (17th century) came to light.

Palazzo San Giorgio

The view across the **Harbour** from the Palazzo San Giorgio should not be missed. One achievement of the Columbus anniversary in 1992 and the harbour Expo site connected with it is the new **Aquarium** (Tuesday, Wednesday, Friday 9.30am–5.30pm, Thursday, Saturday, Sunday 9.30am–7pm) by the Ponte Spinola. More than 50 basins with a combined capacity of 4.5 million litres of water, an exhibition area of 13,000sq m (140,000sq ft) and over 5,000 different aquatic species make this the largest aquarium in Europe, and doubtless the most modern as well. Two subterranean levels contain laboratories, monitoring stations and control panels, guaranteeing the dolphins, seals and other creatures a near-ideal environment.

Expo site at the harbour

To get a good impression of everyday life in the biggest harbour in Italy, take the half-hour-long **harbour round trip** from the Calata Zingara. Permanently visible during the voyage past the long quays is the 117-m (380-ft) high lighthouse known as the *Laterna*, the symbol of the city. Anyone boarding a cruise ship from the Ponte dei

Palazzo San Giorgio: facade detail

Palazzo Spinola:
sumptuous decor

Portici di Sottoripa

Palazzo Spinola: gallery portrait

Mille should take time to admire the attractive art nouveau Stazione Marittima (today it houses the Istituto Idrografico della Marina, which can provide highly detailed maps of the whole Italian coastline) during embarcation.

The Portici di Sottoripa are a fine mixture of old Genoese tradition and busy harbour activity. Their arcades contain several tiny shops and distinctive *friggitorie* ('frying kitchens'). From the Portici, walk down one of the side streets into the Via San Luca and to the **Palazzo Spinola ❻** (both galleries: Tuesday to Saturday 9am–7pm, Sunday 2–7pm, Monday 9am–1pm), originally a medieval building; it received its present-day appearance in 1580. Its stucco facade and richly-decorated interior are typical of 16th- to 18th-century Genoese patrician houses. The building today houses the ★ **Galleria Nazionale di Palazzo Spinola**, and highlights here include a statue of *Justice* by Giovanni Pisano (1313), the painting *Ecce Homo* by Antonello da Messina, a *Praying Madonna* by Joos van Cleve and also *Portrait of a Young Boy* by Anthony Van Dyck. The third and fourth floors are occupied by the Galleria Nazionale della Liguria, which contains a triptych by Joos van Cleve and the *Portrait of Gio Carlo Doria* by Peter Paul Rubens.

On the **Piazza Banchi**, which was the centre of civic and commercial life in Genoa until the 18th century, there are two buildings of particular interest: the late 16th-century Loggia dei Mercanti, which became the first stock exchange in Italy in the 19th century, and the church of San Pietro in Banco, rebuilt during the plague year of 1579 on the first floor of a palazzo.

Genoa's patron saint is St Lawrence, the Roman archdeacon who was grilled to death in 258. Christian iconography always depicts him as a purse, and Italians from elsewhere in the country are rather fond of teasing the (ostensibly avaricious) Genoese for worshipping this particular symbol. The cathedral consecrated to the saint is ★★ **San Lorenzo** ❼, originally constructed in the 9th century before it was destroyed and rebuilt during the early years of the 12th century. The San Giovanni portal on the northern side and the San Gottardo portal on the south facade both date from that time. The mighty cathedral received its present-day appearance in the 13th century, however. French architects designed the severe facade in the style of the cathedrals in Rouen and Chartres, but – like many Ligurian churches – it was also given the characteristic black-and-white stripes. There's an uncomfortably lifelike rendition of the death of St Lawrence on the Gothic main portal with its marble inlay, composite capitals and reliefs. Inside the cathedral, don't miss the ★ **Cappella di San Giovanni Battista** in the south aisle. Genoa's merchants were proud of having succeeded in bringing the remains of John the Baptist back to their city in 1098, but the reliquary only found a proper home in the 15th century when Domenico and Elia Gaggini built this Renaissance chapel. The niches also contain two fine statues by the 16th-century Tuscan sculptor Andrea Sansovino.

Lion at San Lorenzo

Portal detail

23

Tour 2: Marble Magnificence

This tour begins, like the first one, in the Piazza De Ferrari. It proves that travellers of past centuries were quite right to praise Genoa for its impressive streets and magnificent marble palazzi; they justly referred to it as *La Superba*, 'the proud one'.

Right on the square is the neoclassical ★ **Teatro Carlo Felice**, rebuilt between 1987 and 1991, just in time for the Columbus Expo in 1992, after decades of hefty debate. The opera house built by Carlo Barabino in 1827, and destroyed during World War II, has now been restored by the architect Aldo Rossi to new, modern, and not uncontroversial splendour.

Another modernised building is the enormous **Palazzo Ducale** ❽, today the city's Palazzo della Cultura. After ten years' restoration work the building, formerly the seat of government of the Genoese republic, once again radiates 16th-century magnificence. Its noble inner courtyards, the frescoed chapel, the Salone del Gran Consiglio with its frescoes and stucco, the Salone del Minor Consiglio with its glorious paintings, the seven-storeyed tower and the splendid Doge's apartments have all been lovingly restored, as have several adjoining rooms under the roof and down in the basement. A vast space is now available for culture, commerce, craft and gastronomy, and a super-modern, vertical steel ramp designed by architect Giovanni Spalla connects the various storeys.

Palazzo Ducale: interior and detail

Church and
Piazza San Matteo

The nearby **Piazza San Matteo** ❾ is closely connected with Genoa's ubiquitous Doria family. From the 12th century onwards the influential patrician family made this square its own, and today it still retains its medieval atmosphere. Martino Doria had a church of San Matteo built here in 1125, and today's Gothic structure was built above its foundations in 1278 as the private church of the Doria family. The crypt contains the tomb of the great Andrea Doria, designed by the Mannerist sculptor Giovanni Montorsoli. Beside the church are the Palazzo di Branca Doria, the Palazzo di Domenicaccio Doria, the Palazzo Quartara (also Doria property originally) with a relief of *St George and the Dragon* by Giovanni Gagini (1475) on its portal, the mighty Palazzo di Lamba Doria and the Palazzo di Andrea Doria with subtle, Late Gothic elements. What makes the Piazza Matteo so attractive and harmonious are the light and dark stripes running around all the buildings.

Another black-and-white striped structure is the Gothic Palazzo Spinola dei Marmi, which was built in the 15th century – and the Spinola, the Doria, the Grimaldi, the Lomellino, the Lercari and the Pallavicino all bring us to Genoa's largest and most magnificent avenue, the **Via Garibaldi**, once referred to by the much-travelled Madame de Staël as the *Rue des Rois*, or 'street of kings'. Before this street with its eleven palazzi was laid out between 1558 and 1583, Genoa must have seen a great deal of property speculation, forced confiscations and real estate purchases – all very familiar to us today. After three public auctions, the city sold land along a 250-m (820-ft) long stretch of road to five wealthy families, who hired architects to build themselves an elite district, high up on the slope and away from the narrow, dark streets of the Old Town. For once, the Doria family were not among

Via Garibaldi

them: Andrea Doria, who ruled Genoa during the mid-16th century, had settled down in the magnificent Palazzo del Principe in the west of the city instead.

The Pallavicino family commissioned the Cambiaso (No 1) and Carrega Cataldi (No 4) palaces, the Lomellino the Palazzo del Podestà (No 7) and the Palazzo Campanella (No 12), the Lercari the Palazzo Lercari-Parodi (No 3), the Spinola the Palazzo Gambaro (No 2), Palazzo Spinola (No 5), Palazzo Doria (No 6) and the Palazzo Cattaneo-Adorno (Nos 8–10), and the Grimaldi family had an earlier version of the Palazzo Biano (No 11) built here, along with the **Palazzo Tursi**, which today is the Town Hall. Behind the severe facades of these palazzi there are elegant inner courtyards and magnificently decorated rooms, containing many works of art – see for yourself in the Palazzo Rosso or the Palazzo Bianco.

Palazzo Tursi: courtyard and detail

25

During the 17th century, the Brignole Sale family appeared on the scene. Between 1671 and 1677 they had the Palazzo Rosso built on the Via Garibaldi, and today its magnificent halls contain the **Galleria di Palazzo Rosso** ❿ (Tuesday to Saturday 9am–7pm, Sunday 9am–noon, closed Monday), testifying to the taste and culture of this noble family. The highlights here include works by Veronese, Titian, Tintoretto, Caravaggio, Salvatore Rosa, Guercino and Guido Reni, Van Dyck, Dürer, Ribera and Murillo. During the early 18th century the Brignole also converted a Grimaldi palace into the Palazzo Bianco, filling it with sumptuous decoration in the rococo style; today the building houses the **Galleria di Palazzo Bianco** ⓫ (Tuesday to Saturday 9am–7pm, Sunday 9am–noon, closed Monday). Alongside the most famous names in Ligurian art, such as Ludovico Brea, Luca Cambiaso, Bernardo Strozzi and Alessandro Magnasco, there are several Dutch masters including Gérard David, Hugo van der Goes, Jan Provost, Peter Paul Rubens and Antony Van Dyck, and the two Spanish painters Zurbaran and Murillo are also represented.

Anyone in urgent need of a break after all this art can take the *ascensore* (lift) from the Galeria Garibaldi to the Spianata di Casteletto, with its Belvedere Montaldo; the panoramic view across the roofs and towers and the harbour is well worth the detour.

From the Via Garibaldi, cross the Largo della Zecca to reach the 16th-century church of **Santissima Annunziata del Vastato** ⓬. The neoclassical portico leads into a very richly decorated yet harmonious interior, full of marble intarsia work, stucco and frescoes, with 17th-century Genoese altar paintings by Luca Cambiaso, Domenico Piola, Bernardo Strozzi and other local artists.

The Balbi family must have paid a small fortune to build seven family palaces along today's **Via Balbi** between

Palazzo Reale

1602 and 1620. The 17th-century **Palazzo dell'Università** ⑬ was originally a Jesuit college, and its elegant inner courtyard with its loggias and porticoes is well worth a visit. Another place that's always open to the public is the **Palazzo Reale** ⑭ on the other side of the street; it was named after the kings of Savoy and was originally built as a residence for Stefano Balbi between 1643 and 1655. The architect Carlo Fontana extended the building during the 18th century, converting it into a magnificent palazzo, and today it greets visitors in the traditional Genoese colours of red, yellow and green. The baroque and rococo rooms on the first floor house the **Galleria di Palazzo Reale** (daily 9am–1.30pm), with its frescoed hall of mirrors and a fine collection of painting and sculpture.

The park, with its imaginative paving mosaics contrasts pleasantly with the harbour and the **Via di Pré**, situated just below the palace. The busy, cosmopolitan atmosphere of the Via di Pré is quite a contrast after the noble magnificence of the Palazzo Reale. Everything's for sale here, from smuggled cigarettes to T-shirts and electronic appliances, and there are several prostitutes around too. Nevertheless, this place is more of a restaurant district than a red-light one. With all the *trattorie* and *friggitorie*, everything seems very Neapolitan, and the various altars and niches everywhere containing madonnas and saints contrast rather charmingly with the irreverent activities going on just beneath them.

Typical old shop sign

26

Genoa is a harbour city, and Crusaders and pilgrims headed for Jerusalem used to depart from here regularly around 800 or 900 years ago. Thousands of these medieval pilgrims and warriors used to stay in the 11th-century hospice known as the **Commenda di Pré** while they were waiting for ships bound for the Orient. The complex of

Palazzo dell'Università

medieval buildings has been admirably restored, and contains the church of San Giovanni di Pré (1180).

In contrast, the **Palazzo Doria Pamphili** (unfortunately closed to visitors) has lost much of its former splendour. Andrea Doria started building this palazzo when he first came to power in 1528, and five years later it provided accommodation for his patron, Emperor Charles V. Around the middle of the 16th century the magnificent palazzo extended from the sea (with a private Doria harbour) to the hillside. Its halls, filled with frescoes by Perin del Vaga, a student of Raphael, and its hanging gardens, terraces, fountains and statues formed a model for later Genoese Renaissance structures. This 'paradise', as the palazzo and its grounds were once named, has now been broken up and destroyed by the construction of new streets and a railway line, and its future looks bleak to say the least.

Those wishing to end this tour with more pleasant impressions of the city should board the rack railway to Granarolo at the **Piazza Principe**. The view 220m (720ft) above the Old Town, the harbour and the *Lanterna* lighthouse, is most impressive, especially towards evening.

Genoa has hidden secrets

Excursions

The Genoese always felt threatened from the landward side, and they erected the first defensive wall as long ago as AD200. Over the centuries it was extended to adapt to the city's changing needs, and between 1626 and 1632, when Genoa feared an attack by the ever-mightier House of Savoy, the seventh city wall was built: a 12,650-m (41,500-ft) long 'Great Wall' extending across the hilltops around the harbour city, much of which still survives to this day. But even this wasn't enough for the Savoyards, who ruled Genoa from 1815 onwards: they gave the wall at least a dozen forts, and today these are the principal sights of the Parco Urbano delle Mura, opened in 1990 and covering an area of 876 hectares (2,100 acres).

Those eager to do the tour of these forts, either on foot or by mountainbike, should take the 1.5-km (1-mile) long rack railway (the valley station is on the Largo Zecca) up to the 302-m (1,000-ft) high ★ **Righi**, one of the best observation points in the city. Pass the red-brick, 19th-century Torre della Specola to reach the Forte Castellaccio. This fort, restored during the 19th century, was a scene of Guelph-Ghibelline strife in medieval times, and though it is picturesquely situated it is not always open to the public. The Osteria du Richettu, right next to the fort, is a good place for rest and refreshment.

Further north on the Monte Peralto, at the highest point of the city wall, is the mighty **Forte Sperone**. With its towers, embrasures, casemates, powder magazine, and various halls and storage rooms, this is a real citadel; it's open to visitors and is often the scene of cultural events. There's a commanding view from the Forte di Sperone westwards across the forts of Begato and Tenaglia, and the forts of Richelieu, Ratti and Quezzi across to the east.

There are even more military structures to visit. From Forte Sperone you can climb up to the very well-preserved Forte Puin and past the atmospherically situated Forte Fratello Minore to **Forte Diamante**. This fort dates from 1756, and is situated 667m (2,190ft) up in the mountains; it represents the apex of Genoese military engineering. It was erected after Austrian troops had occupied this strategically important ridge above the city wall. On a clear day the view from the star-shaped terrace of this fort extends along the Western Riviera as far as Ventimiglia, with the Ligurian Alps in the distance. Nearby there are some original 'ice-holes': 5-m (18-ft) deep pits into which snow was placed during the winter to provide the city with ice for several months of the year.

The wall is linked by fortresses

Veteran of the times

No other Italian city possesses a long defensive wall in such good condition, and even if military architecture fails to interest you, this tour (4 to 5 hours on foot, 3 hours by mountainbike) also has several breathtaking views. In addition, botanists have found over 900 different species of flora growing wild up here, from the deciduous forests on the northern slopes to aromatic Mediterranean *macchia* on the southern ones.

A city like Genoa that produced Christopher Columbus naturally has a museum devoted to pre-Columbian cultures: the **Museo Americanisto 'Federico Lunardi'** (Tuesday to Saturday 9.30am–noon and 3–5.30pm, Sunday 3 5.30pm, closed Monday) in the formerly 16th-century and now neoclassical Villa Gruber. The exhibition documents the fascinating Maya people, and contains a lot of ethnographic material from many South American countries. The museum also has a good library and photographic exhibition.

The **Villa Doria-Centurione**, an early 16th-century structure in Genoa's suburb of **Pegli**, contains the ★ **Museo Navale** (Tuesday to Thursday 9am–1pm, Friday to Saturday 9am–7pm, 1st and 3rd Sunday in the month 9am–1pm, closed Monday). The exhibition here documents the way the harbour developed, and also the growth of the sailing ship and motor vessel construction industries. The reconstructed caravels in which Columbus sailed to America are fascinating, as are the navigational charts dating from various centuries.

Before the villa suburb of Pegli was turned into a centre of tourism in the middle of the last century, Michael Canzio built the ★ **Villa Durazzo Pallavicini**, and since

Nervi waterfront

29

he was a theatre impresario he also laid out a magnificent ★ **park** all around it with splendid views. This highly romantic location has now been very successfully restored, and the park contains a tropical garden filled with palm trees, a forest of camellias, and various grottoes and fountains. The villa itself houses the **Museo Civico di Archeologia Ligure** (Tuesday to Thursday 9am–7pm, Friday to Saturday 9am–1pm, 2nd and 4th Sunday in the month 9am–1pm, closed Monday), which alongside its archaeological exhibits also has a good ethnological collection.

The eastern suburb of Albaro, best reached on a 15 or a 41 bus, is dominated by the ★ **Villa Giustiniani-Cambiaso**. The Umbrian architect Galeazzo Alessi (1512–72) was influenced by Roman models when he built this Renaissance structure, and it became a basis for many more Genoese villas. Begun in 1548, the building is distinctive for its ground- and first-floor loggias and its scenic location. Today it houses Genoa University's engineering faculty, but the grounds are open to the public.

★ **Nervi**, the villa suburb to the east of Genoa, is famous for the panoramic sea promenade known as the **Passeggiata Anita Garibaldi**, for its well-tended parks (especially the rose garden in the Parco Grimaldi) and for its artistic villas, many of which have now been turned into museums. The **Villa Serra** (Tuesday to Saturday 9am–7pm, Sunday 9am–1pm, closed Monday) contains the Galleria d'Arte Moderna, with a comprehensive collection of Ligurian painting from the 19th and 20th centuries; the **Villa Grimaldi** has a modern art exhibition featuring several multimedia exhibits (Tuesday to Saturday 9am–7pm, Sunday 9am–1pm, closed Monday); and the **Villa Luxuro** (Tuesday to Saturday 9am–1pm, closed Sunday and Monday) houses the museum of the same name with some very fine examples of Genoese furniture and paintings dating from the 17th and 18th centuries.

The patina of ages

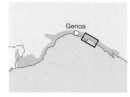

Route 2

Recco – Camogli – Portofino – Santa Margherita – Rapallo – Chiavari – Lavagna (Valle Fontanabuona) – Sestri Levante (approx 50km/30 miles)

Soaking up the sunshine

This route takes us along the Riviera di Levante, or Eastern Riviera, where one wealthy community follows hard on the heels of the next. Camogli's narrow little fishermen's houses have become one of the most-photographed sights in Liguria. Portofino is very exclusive indeed, and Santa Margherita and Rapallo contain artistic villas set amid romantic parks. Zoagli's weavers used to supply princes and cardinals with velvet and brocade. Sestri Levante is very romantically situated in its half-moon shaped bay, and hosts the Hans Andersen fairytale prize annually. Allow yourself one day to cover this route.

The trip begins in **Recco**, and follows the old Roman *Via Aurelia* (highway 1), as much travelled now as it was in antiquity, eastwards from Genoa. This town is a bell-making centre. Ever since the early 19th century, when a few families who had emigrated to Germany returned to their native Liguria, church clocks were manufactured here and bells cast – also in the neighbouring village of Uscio higher up the mountain slope. Today the resort is a small town bereft of character; World War II bombardments destroyed much of its former substance and since then it has never managed to keep up with the more famous towns nearby. Gastronomically, however, Recco really comes into its own: the town is considered to be one of the bastions of Ligurian cuisine. The pancake-like *focacce (see page 79)* here, filled with cheese and then baked in the oven, are generally regarded as the very best in Liguria.

A lot of people come to **Camogli** just to eat. On the second Sunday in May, several hundredweight of fish are fried in 500 litres of oil, inside a frying pan 4m (14ft) in diameter – and there's free fish for everyone. That's not the only reason to visit Camogli, however: with its tall, narrow and colourful fishermen's houses it has become one of the most-photographed towns on the Ligurian Riviera. The reason the facades are so colourful is so that homecoming fishermen could recognise their houses from afar; today there are cafés, restaurants and a sunshade-covered beach along the coast here. The maritime museum, **Museo Marinaro 'Gio Bono Ferrari'** (daily except Tuesday 9am–noon, Wednesday, Saturday and Sunday also 3–6pm), documents the golden age of sea travel during the 19th century, when Camogli had a larger fleet than Genoa

Aspects of Camogli

and would rent it out to warring nations. Around 3,000 sailing ships were built here during that time.

High on a rocky outcrop, the Basilica di Santa Maria Assunta is visible from afar with its neoclassical facade, and the forbidding-looking single tower of the 12th-century Castel Dragone beside it. Inside, the ultra-modern **Acquario Tirrenico** (summer daily 10am–noon and 3–7pm) shows the kind of fish that swim out in the Golfo Paradiso off Camogli – every angler's dream!

Inshore vessels

The ★★ **Benedictine Abbey of San Fruttuoso di Capodimonte** (closed all day Monday and in February) can be reached by ship from Camogli, past the Punta Chiappa, but it also makes for an excellent hike. All that's needed is a sturdy pair of walking boots, three hours' stamina and sureness of foot. There are several magnificent views across the coast and the coastal resorts, and the heady aroma of wild strawberries, gorse, rock roses, rosemary and myrtle makes this tour an unforgettable experience. The hike can also be continued: Portofino is just two hours further away. Sometimes the walking route is the only way of reaching San Fruttuoso anyway, when the sea is too choppy and the ships are forced to remain at anchor in the harbour.

View to San Fruttuoso

The abbey's history stretches far back into the Middle Ages. When the Arabs attacked Spain in the early 8th century, Bishop Prosperus of Tarragona left his country and came to Italy to seek refuge. The sunny hills around Portofino, the luxuriant Mediterranean vegetation and the mild Riviera climate may have reminded him of his lost homeland. To create a suitable home for the relics of St Fructuosus, which the bishop had brought with him, a church and a monastery were soon built. It wasn't safe

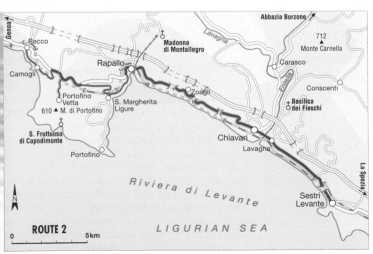

ROUTE 2

0   5km

Monte Portofino

Images of Portofino

from attack by the Saracens, however, and was destroyed in the 10th century before being rebuilt by Benedictines In the 13th century it was renovated by the Doria family and the abbot's palace was added. The Dorias had six of their relatives buried here between 1275 and 1305 because the family church of San Matteo in Genoa was closed for renovation. The Gothic tombs with the vertical 'Doria strip' made of white marble and black stone in the crypt are very impressive. San Fruttuoso is anything but remote these days, however: people lie soaking up the sun only a few yards away. The abbey is no longer as special as it once was, but its location in a (formerly) remote bay and the buildings overgrown with *macchia* vegetation make an excursion here memorable nevertheless.

San Rocco, above Camogli, is a starting-point for hiking trips up ★★ **Monte Portofino**, the highest mountain in the Monte Portofino Nature Reserve. At 610m (2,000ft) Monte Portofino isn't exactly Mount Everest, but the all-round view from the top is still very impressive and on clear days you can even see as far as Elba and Corsica. Botanists have documented more than 700 different plant species up here.

To get to ★★ **Portofino** take the narrow coast road, which is hopelessly jammed from Santa Margherita onwards on summer weekends. The traffic jam has its advantages, however: it gives you longer to admire the villas along the way with their magnificent parks, the rocky cliffs and romantic bays.

The Phoenicians were among the first to realise that the bay of Portofino was the safest natural harbour along the Ligurian coast: it is sheltered from the wind and accessible whatever the weather. The Romans, whose ships set sail for Gaul from here, called the town *Portus Delphini*, the 'dolphin port'. For centuries afterwards it was a small fishing community, but then tourism arrived, and Portofino very soon became a haunt of the rich and famous. Instead of star-spotting down at the yacht harbour, however, take a walk through olive groves to the lighthouse out on the Punta del Capo, past the magnificently situated 12th-century church of San Giorgio (restored in 1950) and also the **Castello di San Giorgio** (daily except Tuesday 10am–5pm), a Genoese bastion erected in around 1600 to defend the Gulf.

A less exclusive and reserved town than Portofino is **Santa Margherita Ligure**, also located at the foot of the Monte di Portofino. The people are young and keen on entertainment, and the hotels cater to all tastes. The palm-lined beach promenade is just the place for a relaxed stroll and an espresso, and beyond the Riviera park with all its exotic plants and statues is the elegant Renaissance villa

of **Durazzo Centurione**. These days this impressive building, which dates from 1560, provides an atmospheric backdrop for chamber music concerts.

Before Santa Margherita Ligure was discovered by the jet set, it was – like all the other Riviera resorts – a small fishing community. Because of this it's a good idea to visit the church of **Sant'Erasmo** and get a feel of local history. The paintings inside show the kinds of dangers to which local fishermen and mariners were often subjected out in the Mediterranean. The small town netted so much fish that it became a desirable place to conquer, however, and Lombards, Saracens and Venetians were all in charge here at different periods in history. In the 16th century the town was taken by the notorious pirate Dragut; today it's been invaded by tourists. The locals have kept tourism successfully in check in some respects, however: the olive groves and oak forests around the town have yet to make way for the anonymous residential complexes that are often such an eyesore elsewhere.

These days the only reminder of **Rapallo**'s dangerous past, when the locals had to fend off pirate attacks, is the small 16th-century **fort** at the harbour. Today this small town, the third 'pearl' along the Golfo del Tigullio after Santa Margherita and Portofino, is a major tourist centre. The palm-lined beach promenade, known as the Lungomare Vittorio Veneto, is lined with old-fashioned art nouveau buildings and charming cafés with glass verandas, and small music groups still perform in the early 20th-century Chiosco della Banda Cittadina. Those interested in liturgical implements will find a collection of processional crosses next door to the church of Santo Stefano in the **Oratorio dei Bianchi** (daily 10am–noon and 3–6pm).

One of the biggest festivals in Rapallo is the day celebrating the Holy Virgin of Montallegro at the beginning

Sea gazing at Santa Margherita Durazzo Centurione

33

Rapallo fort

of July. The whole town makes its way up to the pilgrimage church of **Nostra Signora di Montallegro**, situated 612m (2,000ft) up in the mountains. The church can also be reached by car or by cable car. Its neo-Gothic facade takes some getting used to.

Rapallo, too, lived almost exclusively from fishing until the mid-19th century, when the first tourists came to enjoy its mild winters. While the men were away at sea the womenfolk whiled away the time by lacemaking. The finest of these bobbin lace products can be admired today in the **Museo del Pizzo al Tombolo** (Tuesday, Wednesday, Friday and Saturday 3–6pm, Thursday 10.30am–12.30pm) in the Villa Tigullio.

Rapallo lace

The philosopher Friedrich Nietzsche visited Rapallo several times, and mentions in his autobiography that he actually conceived his greatest work *Also Sprach Zarathustra* ('Thus Spake Zarathustra') while on a walk from Rapallo 'into the heights along the glorious route to Zoagli, past pine trees and with a vast view of the sea'.

Zoagli cemetery

34

The resorts of **Lorsica** and **Zoagli**, on the way to Chiavari, have specialised in clothmaking for centuries, and their products were much sought after by kings and heads of state. The firm of Gaggioli still uses an 18th-century loom to weave its satins. The cloth here is very expensive – it takes one day to produce just 3m (10ft) of it.

Along the road to Chiavari there are several fine views of the coastline between Portofino and Sestri Levante. Soon the 15th-century pilgrimage church of ★ **Madonna delle Grazie** comes into view, perched high above the sea. The interior contains an important fresco cycle by the Ligurian artist Teramo Piaggio, depicting *Scenes from the Life of Christ*; the pink and green pastel tones are most attractive. The *Last Judgement* is by the Ligurian Luca Cambiaso, and was painted in the mid-16th century.

After it has entered the small town of **Chiavari**, the *Via Aurelia* turns into the Via Martiri della Liberazione; the locals simply call it *carrugio dritto* ('straight street'). Today it is still the main shopping street just as it was in medieval times, when Chiavari was built as a fortress town by the Genoese in the 12th century to provide protection against the Fieschi on the other side of the Entella river.

Chiavari: Carrugio dritto

Merchants were the first people to populate Chiavari. The ancient necropolis at the foot of the castle hill proves that the area was settled before the Romans came, in the 8th and 7th centuries BC. The Romans themselves must have noticed very soon just how strategically advantageous Chiavari was as well. The town experienced its golden age during medieval times, however, when it was an important trading post and was so well fortified, with its fortress and walls, that even travellers in the 16th cen-

Local pastime at Sestri Levante

tury considered it to be one of the finest walled towns in Europe. The old walls were razed in the 18th century, however, to make way for new palazzi and housing space.

Today Chiavari is a modern seaside resort. The most impressive structures are the broad **Palazzo Rocca** (1629) with its archaeological museum (Tuesday to Saturday 8am–7.15pm), documenting the finds from the pre-Roman necropolis, the mighty baroque **cathedral**, rebuilt in the 19th century, and the medieval **Palazzo dei Portici Neri** with its impressively high slate plinth.

The bridge across the Entella is all that separates Chiavari from its neighbouring town of **Lavagna**, which has the largest yachting marina in Europe with mooring space for over 1,600 vessels. While the inhabitants of Chiavari were loyal subjects of Genoa, the counts of Fieschi in Lavagna enjoyed centuries of proud, self-confident independence. In the 13th century Pope Hadrian V, a member of this powerful noble family, had a ★★ **Basilica dei Fieschi** built in the nearby village of San Salvatore dei Fieschi. The black-and-white striped facade, the Gothic portal with its lunette fresco, the rose window and the unpretentious interior make it one of the most attractive Romanesque-Gothic structures in Liguria. Along with the Palazzo Comitale next to it, it is a fitting symbol of the power once wielded by the Fieschi family.

35

Basilica dei Fieschi

Sestri Levante is a peaceful seaside resort, and the old part of its centre still retains a very traditional Ligurian atmosphere. The long promenade, which extends the length of the Baia delle Favole ('bay of fairytales'), is just as romantic. At the highest point of the long promontory known as the Isola is the 12th-century church of San Nicolò dell'Isola, and not far away from it is the entrance to the Parco dei Castelli, with the **Marconi Tower** where the physicist Guglielmo Marconi (1874–1937) first experimented with high-frequency radio waves.

Sestri Levante

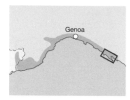

Route 3

★★★ The Cinque Terre

Levanto – Monterosso al Mare – Vernazza – Corniglia – Manarola – Riomaggiore (approx 45km/27 miles)

The five villages that make up the 'Cinque Terre', with their colourful houses bunched closely together, cling to the rocky coast rather like eagles' nests. Lord Byron described this stretch of coast as 'paradise on earth'. Until the last century the locals drank their own wine, cultivated with difficulty up on the steep slopes, and the area was very remote. Today the tourists have arrived in these tiny villages with their steep, narrow streets and miniature squares. The Cinque Terre have so far been spared mass tourism, however, because access to them by car is virtually impossible. This makes conditions even more ideal for the many hikers who come here for the well-marked routes, breathtaking views and comfortable restaurants.

The Cinque Terre are best explored on foot

Riomaggiore

Although it is theoretically possible to visit the Cinque Terre by car, the tiny roads leading to the villages of Monterosso, Vernazza, Corniglia, Manarola and Riomaggiore are narrow, steep and full of bends, and the few car parks have already been claimed by the locals. The Cinque Terre can only be properly appreciated on foot, and for keen

walkers they are one of the best regions in Italy. You can walk from one village to the next and travel back by train to your starting-point, or take the 'Blue Way' (Sentiero Azzurro) high above the sea, through the different villages. In springtime, however, the route tends to be crowded. Possible escape routes in this event would be the Sentiero Rosso No 1, which goes up as high as 700m (2,300ft) but requires the right equipment, or the easier Strada dei Santuari which runs along the slope and connects five pilgrimage churches. Each of the five villages has one of these churches situated above it.

Train at Riomaggiore

It's a good idea to start your tour of the Cinque Terre in **Levanto**, a small resort with quite a few good sights. The Loggia del Comune on the Piazza del Popolo, with its arcades and Romanesque capitals, dates from the 13th century, and the Gothic parish church of Sant'Andrea with its Ligurian striped facade is 30 years older. A bas-relief on the Oratorio di San Giacomo (16th-century) reminds us that the ancient pilgrimage route to Santiago de Compostela passed through Levanto.

The walk from Levanto to Riomaggiore takes around four hours. It's best to travel by train as far as **Monterosso al Mare**. The special Cinque Terre atmosphere – houses huddled together, steep alleys, and fishing boats pulled up as far as the village piazza – is rather absent here, but Monterosso still has the only stretch of coast in the vicinity that could be called a beach. The pilgrimage church, built

Monterosso

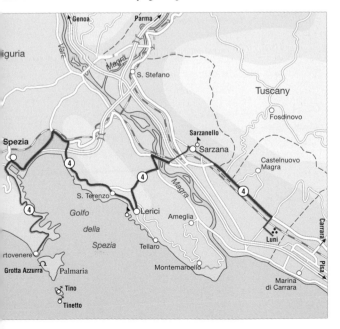

between the 13th and 14th centuries, is the oldest of all the villages. **San Giovanni Battista** is Gothic, and its consecration to John the Baptist is a reminder that this stretch of coast was held by Genoa from 1276 onwards. The artists who came here were also Genoese: the works of 16th- and 17th-century Luca Cambiaso, Bernardo Castello and Bernardo Strozzi can be admired in the Capuchin church of San Francesco (1619) up on the slope. One popular destination for those interested in literature is the red-brick villa that once belonged to the poet Eugenio Montale (1896–1981), a native of Liguria, who won the Nobel Prize for Literature in 1975. He spent many summers here during his childhood and youth.

The Sentiero Azzurro (No 2, with the blue-and-white markings) to Riomaggiore still follows the old medieval routes that were used for transporting goods. Tiny gardens full of greenery, ancient olive groves and carefully-tended vineyards line the route, which provides fascinating views across breathtaking stretches of coastline. The soil on the terraces was brought here with great difficulty, and can often be washed downhill again by heavy rainfall.

Vernazza

The most attractive of the Cinque Terre, **Vernazza**, comes into view. Its buildings all seem to form part of one single labyrinthine structure; narrow streets lead past portals with reliefs, and the whole village is dominated by a medieval round tower, which like the rectangular Saracen tower by the harbour has long outlived its usefulness. The locals usually tend to congregate in the small piazza behind the 14th-century parish church of **Santa Margherita d'Antiocha**, right beside the harbour; its octagonal bell-tower is a distinctive feature of the village.

Unlike the other villages, **Corniglia** does not lie next to the sea but instead extends along a 100-m (330-ft) high outcrop that resembles the prow of a ship. Corniglia is not a fishing village but a wine village, and famed for its full-bodied white known as *Schiacettrà*, which is very difficult to find in the shops. No less delicious is the *Cinque Terre* DOC white wine, also made from Albarola, Bosco and Vermentino grapes. The parish church of **San Pietro**, built in 1334 above the remains of an 11th-century chapel, has a fine Carrara marble rose window and a Gothic portal with a lunette decorated with reliefs. The view from the Belvedere terrace is almost dizzying; there are 377 steps leading down to coast.

Corniglia vineyards
San Pietro

At the railway station at the foot of the steps, the walk continues to **Manarola.** The pink, brown, yellow and light-green houses Paul Klee enjoyed so much are huddled tightly together, almost as if frightened of losing their balance and toppling over the steep grey rock face into the sea below. There's a Gothic parish church here, too: **San Lorenzo**, built in the 14th century, with its marble rose window. The piazza in Manarola is so small and the harbour so tiny that the colourful fishing boats have to be pulled up on to the land.

The last section of this route takes us to **Riomaggiore**. The **Via dell'Amore** connects Manarola with the last of the five villages via a comfortable flight of steps hewn out of the vertical rock face. This route was laid out in the 1930s – and not for romantic walks in the moonlight but to provide quick access to a nearby powder magazine. Even though this village can be reached by road from La Spezia, the whole place is still redolent of times past. One of the first tourists to come to Riomaggiore was the painter Telemaco Signorini, the leading representative of the Italian 'Macchiaioli' art movement, which was devoted to Impressionist painting in natural surroundings. The main street of Riomaggiore from the station to the church is named after him. The Gothic church of **San Giovanni Battista** was the last of the Cinque Terre churches to be built, and dates from around 1340.

Via dell'Amore

For the experienced there is a good hike from Levanto to Riomaggiore along the **Alta Via delle Cinque Terre** which follows the ridge between the Vara Valley and the Ligurian Sea. The whole mountain tour takes eight or nine hours to complete, and the right equipment is essential. It first leads to the scenic Punta Mesco near Monterosso, then to the 330-m (1,000-ft) high Colla di Gritta and the pilgrimage church of Madonna di Soviore (which also provides food and lodging). From here follow route number one, which reaches its highest elevation at the Sella di Malpertuso (780m/2,500ft) and provides a good impression of Liguria's 'two faces': the blue sea on one side, and the green, lonely mountains on the other. And along the path itself, providing an attractive contrast, there are red and white wild strawberry flowers, and yellow gorse.

39

Some people prefer the beach

Manarola

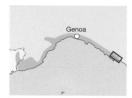

Route 4

Harbours Past and Present

Portovenere – La Spezia – Lerici – Sarzana – Luni
(approx 85km (52 miles) *See map p37*

La Spezia has been one of the chief naval ports of Italy for the past 150 years, and its naval arsenal has given it a military feel; several battles took place here in past centuries too, most of them centred round the medieval castle of Lerici. Today, however, La Spezia and the region around it are far less well-known for past deeds of valour than for astonishingly beautiful landscape. Several famous Romantics lived here at different times, including Lord Byron, Percy Bysshe Shelley, and the Swiss painter Arnold Böcklin. Shelley later lost his life in a tragic boating accident off Livorno.

Portovenere, formerly a pirates' lair, is an incredibly picturesque Italian village. Sarzana, a popular meeting-place for antiques dealers from all over Italy, is dominated by a Medici fortress. International trade flourished in Luni around 2,000 years ago; today only atmospheric ruins remain of the Romans' greatest marble harbour. This route needs a whole day.

40

Portovenere – a safe harbour

Experienced seafarers as they were, the medieval Genoese knew a safe harbour when they saw one. When they purchased **Portovenere** in 1113 they gave this small fishing village enough fortifications to withstand even the worst pirate attack. As a Genoese border post, Portovenere had to be prepared for enemy attack at any time; it was most likely to come from either pirates or from the Pisan castle in Lerici just across the Gulf. This is why the houses in Portovenere form a wall along the shore, and also why the streets are so narrow: they could be closed off within seconds and bolted shut. If conditions got really dangerous, the cliffs could be smeared with tallow to make them slippery, and the women would pour boiling oil or tar over the heads of the enemy. Simple – but effective.

Genoa knew just how strategically important Portovenere was, and treated it with great respect over the centuries. The **castle**, built in 1162 and extended in the 16th and 17th centuries, dominates the town. The Romanesque church of **San Lorenzo** was built even earlier, and was consecrated in 1830 by Pope Innocent II; later it received Gothic and Renaissance additions. There is a fine *Martyrdom of St Lawrence* in the lunette on the main portal. A nocturnal procession to the church takes place on 17 August every year, and the building looks most impressive by torchlight.

The annual procession on 29 June to the church of **San Pietro** is no less impressive. The church is splendidly situated on a rocky cape, and dates from 1250. Its four-arched loggia was added later, and affords a magnificent view of the Cinque Terre as far as Punta Mesco. Beneath it, at the foot of the hill, the Grotta Byron commemorates the great English Romantic poet, who would often come here after a long swim to declaim his verse loudly.

San Pietro

Room with a view

A long flight of steps leads back to the colourful bustle of the Calata Doria at the harbour. Narrow alleys lead from here to the Via Capellini, the picturesque main street, where several elegant slate and marble house portals can still be seen today.

One real must for anyone visiting Portovenere is the 10-minute boat trip out to the ★ **Isola Palmaria**, a rocky island full of caves and covered with macchia, where the ruins of several Stone Age dwellings have recently been discovered. The remains of the 11th-century Abbey of San Venerio are situated on the far smaller **Isola del Tino**, which may only be visited for the Festival of St Venerius on 13 September and the following Sunday.

When Napoleon conquered Liguria in 1797, he was particularly delighted by **La Spezia**, which at that time was a fishing community with around 3,000 inhabitants: 'It is the finest harbour in the world, better fortified even than Toulon, and can be defended just as easily from the land as from the sea.' France's emperor had ambitious plans for the town: he wanted to turn it into a military harbour and increase its population by 12,000. More important considerations and the vagaries of politics left him no time to implement this, however, and the idea was only taken up again in 1860 by the new Kingdom of Italy. La Spezia was given an arsenal and then a trading harbour. Today the

La Spezia: elegant arcades

The promenade

town is the second-largest in Liguria (pop. 109,000) and the most important naval base in Italy. Ferries also sail from here to Corsica during the summer. From the point of view of tourism, however, La Spezia isn't all that inviting; the place is modern and largely anonymous.

Naval heritage

Stelae in the Museo Civico

Some sights are definitely worth seeing, though. Beside the arsenal is the ★★ **Museo Tecnico Navale** (Tuesday, Wednesday, Thursday, Saturday 9am–noon and 2–6pm, Monday and Friday 2–6pm), with its fascinating models of Roman and Greek triremes and galleys, caravels of the type used by the Ligurian Christopher Columbus to discover the New World, Bourbon sailing ships and also 20th-century Italian motor vessels. The collection of ships' figureheads is just as fascinating: the barebreasted *Atlanta*, discovered in the Atlantic in 1864, must have turned quite a few heads on board. Another museum, the **Museo Civico** (Tuesday to Saturday 8.30am–1pm and 2–7pm, Sunday 9am–1pm), documents the distant past. The archaeological collection here includes the Bronze-Age ★★ **stelae** that were discovered in the nearby Lunigiana: stone statues of men and women found on the bed of the River Magra. There are also several Roman remains from Luni, including impressive busts and floor mosaics.

The mighty **Castello San Giorgio** was built in the 12th century by the then powerful Fischi family, and altered and extended by the Genoese in the 14th and 17th centuries. The place is still very forbidding today. At the foot of the hill is the church of **Santa Maria Assunta**. The magnificent *Coronation of the Virgin* terracotta inside by Andrea della Robbia (1500) makes up a bit for the fact that the building had to surrender its cathedral status to the church of **Cristo Re**. This new cathedral, with its circular ground-plan, was designed by architect Adalberto

Libera (1903–63), a leading proponent of the Rationalist movement during the 1920s and 30s. La Spezia has quite a few examples of modern art, in fact: the Quartiere Umberto I, north of the Museo Civico, was laid out as a working men's residential community during the 19th century, in imitation of the French *cités ouvrières* and the Krupp community in Essen.

Cristo Re Cathedral

The broad bay off La Spezia is also known as the 'Gulf of Poets'; the villages on its east side with their rows of picturesque houses and pretty landscape attracted quite a number of romantically-inclined souls during the 19th century. The Swiss painter Arnold Böcklin and the two English poets Byron and Shelley all stayed in **San Terenzo**. In June 1822 Shelley began working on *The Triumph of Life* here, and it was at the beginning of July that he drowned in a boating accident after visiting his fellow writers Byron and Leigh Hunt. His body was washed ashore on 18 July, and was cremated at sea one month later. The Casa Magni, from which Shelley embarked on his tragic journey, contains a small museum devoted to his life and work until recently, but its future is now uncertain since the house was recently sold.

43

The construction boom from tourism has turned San Terenzo and **Lerici** into one large community, and robbed both towns of much of their individual charm. Lerici is dominated by its imposing medieval **castle** (April to October daily 9.30am–12.30pm and 3.30–7pm; July and August until 9pm; otherwise Saturday and Sunday only, 9.30am–12.30pm and 2–5pm), which was built by the Pisans in 1241 as a counterbalance to the Genoese fortifications in Portovenere. The Pisans' good fortune didn't last long, however: the castle was firmly in their Genoese rivals' hands by 1256. An inscription on the entrance portal to the Gothic castle chapel of Sant'Anastasia glorifies this victory.

Lerici

There are several tiny bays and atmospheric caverns and grottoes along the coast between Lerici and **Tellaro**, which still retains all the charm of a traditional Ligurian fishing village, with its impressive church and colourful houses. D.H. Lawrence lived from 1913 to 1914 in nearby Fiascherino, which at that time was very remote.

Tellaro church

Situated on its rocky point, **Montemarcello** faces the bay like a ship's figurehead. Narrow streets between the grey and pink houses, the smell of jasmine and a magnificent view have attracted many Milan VIPs and intellectuals here, and several old mills, farmhouses and medieval watchtowers have now been converted into desirable residences.

The strategic importance of the foothills was well-known as long ago as Roman days, when the Romans defended their marble quarry at Luni from here; in me-

Sarzana

Sarzana citadel and fortress

dieval times Montemarcello was a base during the battles against the Saracens, and in World War II the Germans used it to supervise the nearby 'Gothic Line'.

Ameglia can either be reached along a mountain road, or via the coastal resort of **Bocca di Magra,** which for years was the home of the Italian writer Elio Vittorini. Tall, narrow farmhouses and fishermen's cottages dating from the past three centuries are clustered round the castle hill, and from the square in front of the church there is a superb view of the Plain of Luni and the marble-white Apuan Alps across in Tuscany. Ameglia is another Roman foundation, and in 963, during the reign of Emperor Otto I, it was mentioned in a document as the official seat of the bishops of Luni. Visitors should note that Ameglia's restaurants enjoy a high reputation.

The town of **Sarzana** might never have achieved its present-day importance if people hadn't fled here from the nearby marshland of Luni, from the 11th century onwards. In 1204 Luni had to surrender its bishopric to Sarzana too, and from that moment on the town achieved unparalleled popularity with Pisa, Lucca, Genoa, Milan and Florence for its favourable military and commercial location. The mighty **Citadel** was built on the orders of Lorenzo the Magnificent in 1488, and the architects involved in its construction included the great Renaissance fortress builder Giuliano da Sangallo. The fortress of Sarzanello, situated on a mound to the northwest of the town, is even more impressive: built on a triangular ground-plan, it still retains its original forbidding appearance despite much restoration. The fortress is now used for cultural rather than military purposes.

The old part of town is also distinctive for its Tuscan architecture. The Romanesque-Gothic ★ **cathedral of**

Santa Maria Assunta (13th-/15th-century) with the monument to Sarzana's most famous son, Pope Nicholas V, contains a collection of fine works of art that includes the ★ *Cross of Master Guglielmo* (1138, being restored at present) and two 15th-century marble winged altars by Leonardo Riccomanni from Pietrasanta in Tuscany.

Today Sarzana is a small, sleepy town, but in past centuries conditions were very different. During medieval times, pilgrims passed through here along the *Via Francigena* to Rome and the Holy Land. Today pedlars come here to Sarzana every August from all over Italy to spread out their wares at the street market *(Soffita in Strada)*, while the town's antiques dealers exhibit valuable items in the Palazzo degli Studi.

Sarzana's most famous citizen was probably Napoleon Bonaparte, who lived in the area with his family before they emigrated to Corsica in 1529.

★ **Luni** lies less than a mile from the Tuscan-Ligurian border. The Romans laid it out originally as a fortress in their fight against the Ligurians during the 2nd century BC, and it soon developed into a busy harbour. The merchandise traded here included wine and cheese from the (Tuscan) Lunigiana, wood from the dense Apennine forests, and above all marble from the Apuan Alps – all of it shipped directly to Rome. Carrara and its marble quarries are just a stone's throw away, and the pure, snow-white marble from the Apuan Alps – or *Lunae Montes* as they were then known – was very much in demand in Rome. The construction boom vanished with the decay and fall of the Roman Empire, however, and demand for marble from Luni slackened off. Over the centuries the Magra river washed so much alluvial material down to its delta that Luni began to silt up. Malaria broke out in the marshy areas around the town, and most of the population moved to Sarzana, leaving their once-glorious marble harbour behind. Excavations in 1837 revealed a forum, a theatre, an amphitheatre, a temple of Diana and several magnificent villas with frescoes and mosaic floors such as the Casa dei Mosaici (3rd century AD) and the Casa degli Affreschi.

The **Museo Archeologico Nazionale** (daily 9am–7pm) with its collection of finds from recent excavations could have been better located, however: it's right at the centre of the ancient town. Statues and busts of emperors testify to the high artistic level of the ancient harbour of Luni, which today lies 2km (1 mile) from the sea. The museum also provides fascinating insights into marble quarrying and marble working during Roman times. The amphitheatre in the ruined city once held 5,000 spectators; it is now used as an atmospheric venue in the summer months for theatre and ballet performances.

Cathedral detail

Antiques market

45

Museum of Archaeology: bust of an emperor

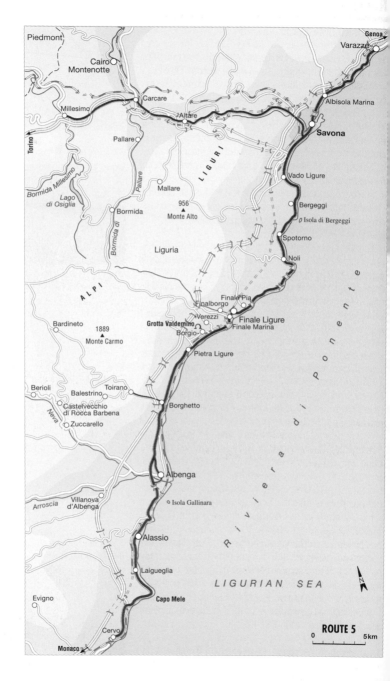

Route 5

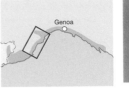

Art, Ceramics and Chamber Music

Varazze – Albisola – Savona (Millesimo) – Spotorno – Noli – Finale Ligure – Verezzi – Toirano – Albenga – Alassio – Laigueglia – Cervo (100km/62 miles not including excursion inland)

Today's ceramic artists in Albisola are so prolific that the entire beach promenade is paved with their work. Noli and also the many-towered town of Albenga were enriched by medieval artists; the fine piazza in Verezzi is transformed into an open-air theatre in the summer; and the square outside the church in Cervo is used for international chamber music performances. Culture plays an important role in the towns and villages along this route, which also leads back into the dim prehistoric past inside the Caves of Toirano. The provincial capital of Savona is extremely modern, and Fiats and Lancias are exported around the world from its harbour. Allow two days for this trip – or three if you feel like exploring the mountains inland.

Dinghy sailors at Varazze

Sant'Ambrogio ruins

The town of **Varazze** not only possesses a yachtbuilding centre and a mile-long sandy beach but also the parish church of **Sant'Ambrogio**, built above the foundations of a previous Romanesque-Gothic structure. All that remains of the latter today is the campanile. The church contains a polyptych of *St Ambrose with Divine and Music-Making Angels* by the Genoese artist Giovanni Barbagelata (1500) and also a *Virgin* by the 16th-century Ligurian painter Luca Cambiaso.

The main attraction of Varazze, however, is the nearby ★ **Monte Beigua Nature Reserve**, only a 20-km (12-mile) drive away. Monte Beigua itself is 1,287m (4,220ft) high, and the trip here is worthwhile for the magnificent panoramic view from the top alone, which on a clear day extends northwards to Monte Rosa and southwards as far as Corsica. This mountain massif is only 6km (4 miles) or so from the sea as the crow flies, and the contrast between southward-facing Mediterranean vegetation and northward-facing mountain flora is nowhere more apparent. The bare, serpentine rock walls have provided many Ligurian architects with construction material over the centuries, and several unique ★★ **cave drawings** have also been discovered in the region which are thought to be 5,000–6,000 years old.

The work of more modern artists is one of the most striking features of **Albisola Marina**, which can be reached via the resort of Celle Ligure. The local enthusiasm for ce-

Albisola Marina

Tile designs on the promenade

Ceramics on sale

ramics has resulted in a series of coloured tiles along the Lungomare degli Artisti, the beach promenade that runs parallel to the *Via Aurelia*. This multi-coloured tiled carpet is the work of contemporary Italian artists such as Giuseppe Capogrossi, Roberto Crippa, Agenore Fabbri, Lucio Fontana and Aligi Sassu, and also the Dane Asger Jorn and the Cuban Wifredo Lam.

The ceramic artists in Albisola can still be seen at work today, because it's been an unbroken tradition since the 16th century. The history of the ceramics industry is documented in the **Museo del Centro Ligure per la Storia della Ceramica** (daily except Tuesday 3–7pm) in the Villa Fariggiana. Ceramics are also the main focal point inside the Manlio Trucco (daily except Sunday 10am–noon). In the upper part of Albisola, the Villa Gavotti gives a fascinating glimpse of what life was like for the Ligurian nobility during the 18th century.

A good detour for gourmets here leads up to the 23-km (14-mile) distant tourist town of **Sassello**, situated 405m (1,300ft) up in the mountains: it's famous for its small almond-flavoured biscuits called *Amaretti*. The route also leads past the rather inconspicuous-looking village of **Stella**, where the politician Sandro Pertini (1896–1990) was born and also lies buried. He was persecuted and imprisoned under the Italian Fascist regime but ended up as the president of Italy from 1978 to 1985, a success partly attributed to his unconventional style.

Savona has been an important harbour town for over 2,000 years, and today is more important than ever in its role as the export harbour for Fiat and Lancia cars, all of which are transported here from Turin for sale across the world.

The history of this town, which today has 67,000 inhabitants, has always been inextricably linked with the

Savona: prosperity of the past

48

nearby and far smaller community of Vado Ligure. Whenever one of the two experienced an economic upswing the other suffered. During the Punic Wars, Savona was popular when it backed Hannibal, but otherwise Vado enjoyed Roman support; during the Early Middle Ages it was Savona's turn again, then Vado's, until King Berengar II made Savona the capital of part of the Ivrea Marches in the 10th century, henceforth banning Vado to its subsidiary role. Despite its success, Savona was still a prime target during wartime: in the early 16th century its harbour was filled in by the Genoese, who feared competition, and in World War II the town suffered very heavily from aerial bombardment.

Fans of contemporary architecture should go to the western part of town and take a look at the main railway station (1960) and the Palazzo della Provincia (1964), both of them designed by the famous Italian architect Pier Luigi Nervi (1891–1979). Otherwise a walk through the old town by the harbour suffices to gain a good impression of what Savona has to offer. By the harbour there are still three towers dating from the Middle Ages; one of them, the **Torre de Leon Pancaldo**, is named after the mariner

Torre de Leon Pancaldo   49

from Savona who accompanied Magellan on his voyage round the world in 1521. In the 15th century the Della Rovere family grew very powerful, and Sixtus IV and Julius II (the two family members who became popes) were very generous to their native town. Sixtus IV had a **Sistine Chapel** built on to the cathedral cloister to house his parents' tombs; it received its present-day rococo glory in the 17th century. In 1495 Giuliano della Rovere, later to become Pope Julius II, commissioned the Tuscan architect Giulio da Sangallo to build the Palazzo della Rovere (no public admission). Around a century later the cathedral was built, but the Genoese conquered Savona in 1528 and had the entire area, including the cathedral and the episcopal palace, razed to the ground. In its place they built the mighty **Fortezza del Priamar**, to dissuade their new subjects from contemplating any thoughts of rebellion.

Sistine Chapel

Fortezza del Priamar

The town's cathedral was rebuilt at another location. Inside it as well as in the adjoining Museo del Tesoro della Catedrale, where the cathedral treasure is kept, there are some magnificently carved early 16th-century choir stalls, valuable gold and silver artefacts and also works by the Renaissance painters Ludovico Brea, Luca Cambiaso and Albertino Piazza. The nearby rococo chapel of Nostra Signora di Castello contains a polyptych by Vincenzo Foppa and Ludovico Brea. Fans of ceramics will find an extensive collection of 16th- to 19th-century exhibits in the ★ **Pinacoteca Civica**, along with two very impressive Late Medieval versions of the *Crucifixion* (Monday to Saturday 8.30am–12.30pm).

To get a proper feel of Savona, take a stroll along the main shopping street, the Via Paleocapa, and down its medieval side-streets – or walk up to the Fortezza del Priamar. The hill on which it stands has been central to the town's history: Romans, Byzantines and Lombards all fortified it, and the people of Savona successfully defended themselves from here against attacks by the Saracens, the French and the Milanese. They were less successful in their fight against the Genoese, who built the present-day fortress in 1542. The **Museo Archeologico** (Tuesday to Saturday 10am–12.30pm and 3–6pm, Sunday 3–6pm) contains an impressive necropolis and also several North African mosaic floors dating from the 3rd and 4th centuries, while the Museo Sandro Pertini has exhibitions of drawings and sketches by contemporary Italian artists.

If all that art and culture has tired you out, why not follow the locals' example and set off on an early-morning visit to the Mercato Coperto near the harbour? The *Trippe in brodo*, tripe soup, is popular with the sailors here.

Altare glass

Murano Glass is famous the world over, but has anyone heard of 'Altare Glass'? Glass production in **Altare**, a village 15km (9 miles) outside Savona, may indeed be even older than the Venetian variety. It was probably introduced here in the 11th century by Flemish masters, but never achieved the international reputation of its Venetian competitors. Alongside the larger factories there are still several small establishments here where glass is blown by hand. The **Museo del Vetro** (Monday to Saturday 3–6pm) contains several exhibits of locally produced glassware, including a bottle 130cm (51 inches) high which is thought to be the largest in the world.

Millesimo

Travel via Ferrania now for another 15km (9 miles) as far as the village of **Millesimo**. Like many communities inland, it is dominated by a Carretto castle, and its arcaded main square with the originally Romanesque church of Santa Maria extra Muros (15th-century fresco fragments) is a romantic place for a rendezvous.

The best way of getting back to the coast at this point is to drive along the Turin-Savona motorway, which is very scenic all the way to **Vado Ligure**. This harbour for crude oil products also contains a **Museo Civico** (Monday, Thursday and Saturday 9.45am–12.45pm; Tuesday, Wednesday, Thursday and Friday 3–6.30pm) with Roman and medieval finds, as well as several works by the contemporary sculptor Arturo Martini (1889–1947).

The route continues now via Bergeggi with its island of the same name (now a nature reserve, but unfortunately closed to the public), and past the very built-up resort of

Spotorno with its medieval castle, to arrive in **Noli**. This little resort was once a focal point of international politics. After Noli had grown rich and influential during the First Crusade in 1097 it became an independent maritime republic shortly afterwards, in the 12th century. During the years that followed, Noli – the smallest maritime republic in Italy – fought on the Genoese side against Venice and Pisa, and it was only 600 years later, in 1797, that it finally lost its independence to Napoleon. The Loggia della Repubblica still commemorates Noli's glorious past, as does the 'Regata Storica dei Rioni' which takes place here every year on the second Sunday in September.

Noli has retained its flair more successfully than the other resorts along the Riviera. The 12th-century ruined **castle**, with its fortifications stretching from the castle hill to the town walls, is just as impressively scenic as the ancient streets with their buttressed houses and the five brown towers dating from the 13th and 14th centuries. Noli is thought to have had as many as 70 of these towers during the 13th century, for every shipowner or captain had the right to build a tower house at least 50m (160ft) high. The church of **San Paragorio** is one of the most important Romanesque structures in Liguria. It was built above the ruins of a previous Early Christian building in the mid-11th century. The stone sarcophagus on the northern side of the church still dates from that time. The facade is decorated with arched friezes in the Lombard Romanesque style, and the three-aisled interior contains three irregular apses facing the sea. Highlights here include a Romanesque lectern, a wooden episcopal throne (12th-century), the remains of a 15th-century fresco, and also a remarkable wooden crucifix dating from the 12th century which portrays Christ wearing a tunic.

The cathedral of **San Pietro** (13th- and 16th-century) is also worth a quick visit; its medieval structure is still

Noli castle and fortifications

Local occupations

very much in evidence, despite several early baroque alterations. Just outside the Gothic gate on the eastern side of town is the large lemon-yellow church of **Nostra Signora delle Grazie**, built in the 18th century, with white rococo decoration on its facade. From the square in front of it there is a fine view of Noli and its bay, especially towards evening. Alongside all the art and history, present-day Noli still hasn't lost its original charm either. It has retained a 'fishing village' atmosphere more successfully than the other Ligurian coastal communities. The fishermen here still pull their nets up on to the beach, and sardines in brine from Noli make a good souvenir.

Varigotti

Continue along the *Via Aurelia* now, through **Varigotti** with its colourful houses, as far as ★ **Finale Ligure**, which actually consists of three separate communities: Finale Pia, Finale Marina and Finalborgo. **Finale Marina**, an important trading centre in the old days, is now a modern and well-equipped seaside resort with a nice sandy beach and a palm-tree-lined promenade. In the Piazza Vittorio Emanuele II, an imposing-looking triumphal arch commemorates the visit here by the Spanish-Habsburg heiress Margherita in the year 1666, on her way to Vienna to marry the Austrian Habsburg emperor Leopold I in Vienna. The baroque church of San Giovanni Battista, built above the ruins of an Early Christian basilica dating from the 5th–8th centuries, is surrounded by elegant 16th-, 17th- and 18th-century town houses and palazzi.

During medieval times **Finale Pia** grew up around the church of Santa Maria di Pia; its facade is rococo and its interior baroque, and the only surviving Romanesque-Gothic feature is the 13th-century campanile. The abbey next to it was founded by the Benedictine Order in the 16th century; the monks brought their own ceramic artists with them from Tuscany, and the work here is strongly influenced by the Della Robbia school.

Medieval Finalborgo

The most attractive of the Finales is ★ **Finalborgo**. Its situation a short way inland has spared it the architectural excesses of tourism; indeed, its 15th-century medieval centre is almost completely intact. The town was founded by the margraves of Carretto after an earlier settlement had been completely destroyed during their wars with the Genoese. There is no shortage of picturesque corners here, and vegetable shops and stand-up cafés are housed inside elegant palazzi with stuccoed ceilings. Past and present make an attractive combination here, and there's nothing museum-like about this busy town either. Before you visit one of the restaurants for a *pasta con pesto* (a typical noodle dish with basil sauce which is an absolute must in Finalborgo, a town renowned for its basil), pay a brief visit to the parish church of **San Biagio**. Its Late

Gothic campanile, built on top of one of the old fortification towers, is the town's most famous landmark, and the baroque interior contains some fine 18th-century marble sculpture. A 15-minute walk leads to **Castel Gavone**, an impressive complex of ruins, and all that survives of a mighty 15th-century fortress. The **Torre dei Diamanti**, with its diamond-patterned walls, makes an excellent subject for a photograph, and also contains several interesting fresco fragments.

Castel Gavone with the Torre dei Diamanti

One real must in Finalborgo is a visit to the **Museo Civico del Finale** (summer: Tuesday to Saturday 10am–noon and 3–6pm; October to May: 9am–noon and 2.30–4.30pm; Sunday 9am–noon all year round), housed inside a cloister of the former monastery of Santa Caterina. The collection here documenting the history of the Finalese features Roman and medieval as well as Stone Age and even Ice Age finds, the latter from the numerous caves in the region.

A good way of soaking up the history of this region is to take a short trip from Finale Pia to the **Val Ponci**. The five Roman bridges here dating from the 2nd century (three of them are still in remarkably good condition) show how efficient the Romans were at roadbuilding, even in 'provincial' areas. The *Via Julia Augusta* used to pass this way; it was built in AD13, and restored by the emperor Hadrian (who had the bridges added) in the 2nd century. It is possible to hike from here to the Altopiano delle Manie, a limestone plateau with much fascinating flora and fauna. The earliest inhabitants of Liguria used the caves in this region as long as 300,000 years ago. There are primitive rock drawings on the rockface known as the Ciappo del Sale showing symbolic figures, crosses and abstract human forms. The Romans used this region later as a quarry.

53

There are also several caves in the region around **Borgio-Verezzi**, and the limestone cavern known as the **Grotta Valdemino** (daily except Tuesday 9am–noon and 3–6pm, October to April 9–11.30am and 2.30–5.30pm) with its stalactites is well worth a visit. There are a lot more attractive sights in this double resort (Borgio is by the sea and Verezzi is up on the slope above), however. The parish church in Borgio, for instance, with its magnificent neoclassical facade, and the church of Santo Stefano with its interesting Romanesque-Gothic features.

Borgio-Verezzi: the church

Verezzi, only 200m (650ft) higher up, is like being in a different world entirely. The four tiny localities of Poggio, Piazza, Roccaro and Crosa that go to make it up are almost reminiscent of a medieval Saracen village, with their square houses all huddled together. Piazza, the largest of the four, has a very peaceful Piazza Sant'Agostino where first-class theatre performances are held from mid-

Flower stall

July to the beginning of August against a scenic backdrop. The sparsely-planted slopes with their walled terraces, olive trees, vineyards and almond trees are a feast for the eye. In the evening the lights from the coastal resorts are most spectacular.

Pietra Ligure and Loano are modern and built-up – something relatively unavoidable for small resorts along the narrow Ligurian coast. Their older sections still have a quaint charm of their own, however. **Pietra Ligure** is dominated by its castle (originally medieval, with later alterations), and the Castello in **Loano** is a magnificent palace surrounded by a park, erected by Giovanni Andrea Doria at the beginning of the 17th century. The Doria, who ruled the town almost without interruption from 1477 to 1737, also built the Convento di Monte Carmelo, where they had their family mausoleum until 1793. The four-hour ascent to this attractively situated Carmelite convent is worth it for the views and the landscape alone.

Toirano detail

From the anonymous-looking seaside resort of Borghetto Santo Spirito, a trip to ★★ **Toirano** (3km/2 miles) is a must. There are several magnificent medieval buildings and palazzi with slate portals, but the nearby limestone caverns are the village's real claim to fame. The **Museo Preistorico della Val Varatella** (daily 9am–noon and 2–5pm) contains collections of fossils and primeval implements and ceramics that were discovered in the caves surrounding the town. It's even more fascinating to visit the caves themselves, however. The footsteps of a Cro-Magnon man were discovered in the **Grotta della Bàsura**, or 'Witch's Grotto' (daily 9am–noon and 2–5pm); he lived there 15,000 years ago and fought giant cave bears on a regular basis. The sparkling minerals in the neighbouring **Grotta di Santa Lucia** (daily 9am–noon and 2–5pm) make it a truly magical subterranean cavern.

The Witch's Grotto

The houses in the nearby village of **Balestrino** seem on the point of sliding down the steep slope, and have been deserted by their occupants – a typical example of inland depopulation in Liguria, where steep, eroded slopes make life very difficult if not downright impossible.

Albenga: the baptistry roof

After all the narrowness of the Riviera coast, the sheer expanse of the fertile plain around ★★ **Albenga**, with its fruit and vegetable plantations, comes as quite a surprise. The real highlight of Albenga is not its fruit and vegetable industry, naturally enough, but its medieval architecture: the Early Christian baptistery, the Romanesque-Gothic cathedral, high medieval towers and several old palazzi all combine to produce an absolutely magnificent old town. The entrance to the ★★ **baptistery** is situated at the foot of a flight of steps, some 2m (7ft) beneath today's street level, which has changed due to the numerous floods that have afflicted the town throughout the centuries. The building has ten outer walls, but is octagonal inside, and dates back to the 5th century. An unfinished font stands at the centre of the chapel. Twelves doves encircle the monogram of Christ in a priceless Byzantine mosaic dating from around AD500, decorating the principal apse opposite the entrance. The floral ornamentation on the tomb to the right of the entrance is 8th-century Lombard work. The cathedral of **San Michele** was built at the same time as the baptistery, but received its present appearance after it was rebuilt in the 13th century. Three Renaissance lions guard the Piazzetta dei Leoni outside the main apse.

The cathedral

Albenga was originally founded as *Albium Ingaunum*, and conquered by the Romans in 181BC when they were securing a direct route to Spain. The old part of Albenga has inherited the rectangular Roman grid pattern of streets, but the most important traces of its heritage can be found in its museums. The **Civico Museo** Ingauno (daily except Monday 10am–noon and 3–6pm), housed inside the 14th-century Palazzo Vecchio del Comune, contains several Roman inscriptions and sculptures. The **Museo Navale Romano** (daily except Monday 10am–noon and 3–6pm) also has some fascinating finds. Its collection includes around 10,000 wine amphorae that were once part of the freight of a Roman ship that sank off Albenga during the 1st century BC. In 1925 a fisherman found several of the amphorae in his net, but it was only in 1950 that the cargo, 40m (130ft) down, could finally be brought ashore; the ship itself is still down there to this day.

Maritime motifs in the Naval Museum

55

The **Pontelungo**, a many-arched bridge built across the Centa by the Romans as part of their *Via Aurelia*, was left to decay when the river changed its course but has nevertheless survived the centuries.

The town of **Alassio** has now completely surrendered to tourism. Rather than promoting its ancient monuments and works of art like Albenga, Alassio promotes its mild climate, its long sandy beach and its entertainment centres. The church of Sant'Ambrogio with its fine Renaissance slate portal is almost obscured from view by the colourful bustle in the town centre. Its magnificent baroque interior contains several paintings by Genoese artists of the 16th and 17th centuries. Alassio's main attraction is the Muretto ('little wall'), covered with colourful ceramic tiles portraying well-known stars of stage, screen and literature such as Ernest Hemingway, Louis Armstrong, Dario Fo, Giuseppe Guareschi and Sandro Mazzola.

Alassio lifeguard

Night life in Alassio centres around its main street, the Via XX Settembre, where cafés and restaurants stay open until the early morning hours.

Laigueglia beach and church

Cervo: San Giovanni Battista

The **Isola Gallinara** lies off the coast of Alassio and Albenga. Its wealth of flora and fauna has now made it a regional nature reserve, and because of this it is now closed to public access.

The far more peaceful town of **Laigueglia** is now almost a part of Alassio, but unlike its noisier neighbour it still retains the atmosphere and appearance of a Ligurian fishing village. The majolica tile decoration on the dome of the 18th-century baroque parish church of San Matteo is playfully naive. It's possible to drive from Laigueglia to nearby Colla Micheri, but walking is a better idea. In 1958 Thor Heyerdahl, the famous Norwegian zoologist and anthropologist, fell in love with this tiny village up on the hillside; he bought it, restored it, and now resides here permanently.

Cervo is a real picture-book Ligurian village, high above the sea. The chamber music festival here was founded over 30 years ago by the renowned Hungarian violinist Sandor Vegh, and the concerts are held in the scenic square outside the baroque church of **San Giovanni Battista**. It's quite a crush for the musicians and the audience in this tiny square, which is surrounded by narrow streets, colourful houses and terraces, all set against the backdrop of the sea. The money to build the church came from coral fishing, thanks to which Cervo grew quite prosperous in the 17th century. The marble and stucco interior is magnificent and definitely worth a visit.

Narrow little streets lead up from the church to the Castello. This imposing medieval structure contains the ★ **Museo Etnografico del Ponente Ligure** (Monday to Friday 9am–1pm and 4–8pm, Saturday and Sunday 9am–1pm and 4–6pm), with its fascinating and extensive ethnological collection documenting rural and maritime life in the Cervo region.

Route 6

Olives, Oil and Spaghetti

Imperia – Pontedassio – Pieve di Teco – Triora – Taggia – Arma di Taggia – Bussana (100km/62 miles)

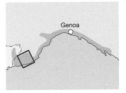

This is definitely a route for gourmets. It begins at the Olive Museum in Oneglia and leads through glorious country-side to Pieve di Teco, formerly a popular rest-stop for medieval salt transporters. As well as being notorious for its witch trials in 1587, Triora is also well-known for its 'Snail Festival', held during late summer every year.

Art fans will also enjoy this route: the parish church and the Dominican monastery in Taggia are decorated with several very valuable old masters. Further along the route, the ruined village of Bussana Vecchia has now become a colony for modern artists, sculptors and potters from all over the world.

Motorists should note that the narrow, winding roads inland require patience and skill, especially the stretch between Pieve di Teco and Triora. Because of this it's best to plan at least two days for the trip.

57

Imperia actually consists of two towns: the medieval Porto Maurizio, up on a hill on the western side of the Impero delta, and the more modern (and prosperous) Oneglia to the east. The two communities were joined together in 1923 after centuries of rivalry: Porto Maurizio had always been loyal to Genoa, while Oneglia was a harbour for the House of Savoy. To avoid ruffled feelings, the town hall and post office are situated exactly halfway between the two ex-towns. Imperia was named after the Impero river which had formerly separated its two halves.

Imperia: Porto Maurizio

The inhabitants of **Porto Maurizio** were relying on a long period of economic prosperity when they began building the mighty cathedral of San Maurizio in the late 18th century, but the turmoil of the Napoleonic era soon dashed their hopes. Porto Maurizio never expanded any further than the hills its huddled houses still occupy, and the neoclassical **cathedral** looks incongruously large and pompous. Construction work only ended in 1838, rather than in 1781 as originally planned, after the oversized cupola had collapsed and been replaced by a smaller one. The interior contains several paintings by Gregorio De Ferrari and Domenico Piola, two respected Ligurian artists of the early 18th century who paved the way from baroque heaviness to the light and playful rococo style.

The ★ **Museo Navale Internazionale del Ponente Ligure** (Wednesday to Saturday 4–7.30pm, July and August also 9–11pm), housed together with the Pinacoteca Civica

The cathedral

Parasio

inside a neoclassical building on the cathedral square, documents the history of seafaring on the Western Riviera. There are over 130 models of sailing ships ancient and modern here, together with a collection of moving votive pictures.

Narrow streets right next to the cathedral lead into the **Parasio** (probably derived from the Roman *palatium*), the old section of town. The originally medieval church of San Pietro, which contains some fine frescoes, rests on the remains of the old town wall. There's a good view across the Riviera from the church parapet, and the loggia-lined promenade of the 18th-century Convento di Santa Chiara – also built on the ruined town wall – is just a short walk

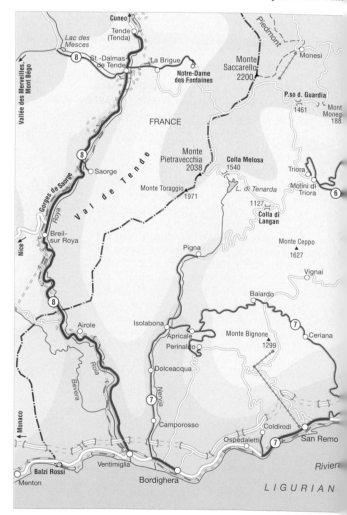

away. Elegant slate portals and sculpture on the palazzi and townhouses here make it clear that Porto Maurizio's Parasio has certainly seen better days.

If you want to experience some real Ligurian atmosphere, have a look at the **Borgo Foce** quarter down by the water below the Paraiso. Here you can watch fishermen as they repair their nets or stroll around the nearby Borgo Marina, which was built around a medieval hospice belonging to the Knights of Malta.

There's a good detour (10km/6 miles) from Porto Maurizio to the pilgrimage church of ★ **Madonna delle Grazie**, built above the spot where, according to the legend, a dumb shepherd girl suddenly began to speak after a vi-

Parasio's past prosperity

Parasio – the old section of town

ROUTES 6–8

N

0   5km

Carli

Pontedassio

Pieve di Teco: Corso Ponzoni

sion of the Virgin. Construction work began on this idyllically situated church in 1450, and its frescoes were painted by the brothers Tomaso and Matteo Biazaci in 1483. The realistic depiction of hell and its torments must have had a salutary effect on sinners over the centuries.

The other half of Imperia, **Oneglia**, may not be as historically important as Porto Maurizio, but it does pride itself on having once been the home town of Andrea Doria (1466–1569, *see page 11*), the capricious soldier of fortune and politician who gave Genoa 30 years of freedom and independence. The birthplace of this somewhat controversial hero lies in the Via – yes, you guessed it – Andrea Doria.

Just behind the railway station in Oneglia the famous olive-oil manufacturing firm of Carli has set up a state-of-the-art **Museo dell'Olivo** (daily except Tuesday and Sunday 9am–noon and 3–6pm) in an art nouveau villa. The ten departments inside document the history of the ancient art of olive cultivation, which grew so important in the Mediterranean region during medieval times that even today 95 percent of olive oil production still takes place there. Botanical and medicinal information, various oil mills and oil presses and the reconstructed cargo hold of an Ancient Roman freighter are just some of the themes and sights of this fascinating museum.

Continuing along the valley of the River Impero in the Ligurian hinterland, it is well worth taking time to explore some of the villages that lie off the main road. There are **Bestagno** and **Villa Guardia** above Pontedassio, both of which date back to the middle ages, and **Borgomaro** which was once an important centre for the marketing and distribution of olive oil.

Proof that the remote towns and villages further inland were once of far greater importance is amply provided by **Pieve di Teco**. The neoclassical parish church of **San Giovanni Battista** was built between 1792 and 1806 by the Lombard master architect Gaetano Cantone, who also designed the cathedral in Porto Maurizio and the parish church in Pietra Ligure. This region earned the money to pay for its works of art from its strategic situation on the much-travelled salt routes, which ran from the sea across the Ligurian Alps and Apennine passes to the plain of Piedmont and Lombardy and intersected in Pieve di Teco. The town was founded in 1233 and contained paper mills, silk factories, ropemaking workshops and weaving centres, and the caravans that transported precious salt from the Ligurian coast across the mountains were very happy to take a break in the shade of the trees along the **Corso Ponzoni**. Elegant palazzi and artistically decorated slate portals testify to the town's former importance.

Pieve di Teco: the clocktower

61

Keen hikers visiting Liguria will hardly be able to resist taking a detour from Pieve di Teco to the mountain village of **Monesi** (1,310m/4,300ft above sea level), and scaling the highest mountain in Liguria, **Monte Saccarello** (2,200m/7,200ft). It takes three hours to get to the summit from Monesi. The northern slopes of the mountain are covered with Alpine roses every summer, and its strategic location between Italy and France meant that it was given a comprehensive network of footpaths between the two World Wars – making things easy for hikers and climbers.

A hiker's paradise

A winding road, rather steep in places, leads from Pieve di Teco via the mountain village of Rezzo to Molini di Triora and Triora. **Molini di Triora** is named after the 23 mills (Italian: *mulini*) formerly in operation here. This sleepy little town is an ideal base for excursions and hiking trips; motorists can travel to the broad plain up on the Colle di Langan (1,127m/3,700ft), or to the Colle Melosa (1,540m/5,052ft) where the Franco Allavena refuge hut is located (the key is available from the CAI in Bordighera). For potholing enthusiasts there are numerous limestone caverns in the Pietra Vecchia Toraggio massif, and mountain climbers can test their mettle on the ★ **Sentiero degli Alpini**, a path hewn out of vertical limestone walls by Italian soldiers between 1936 and 1938. The plan here was to build a secret supply route just in case war broke out between Italy and France – which of course it did soon afterwards. This walk, which should also include a hike around the Monte Pietravecchia (2,038m/6,686ft), is extremely scenic and takes about six hours to cover completely.

Witches, superstition and the black arts are all inextricably linked with **Triora**. In 1587, when a famine broke out in the region, a scapegoat was sought – and found in the shape of 200 women, all of whom were accused of witchcraft and tried in Genoa. Many were tortured, some

Triora

pretended they met the devil every night to save their lives, and around 15 were condemned to death. The **Museo Etnografico Alta Valle Argentina** (summer daily 3.30–6.30pm; winter Sundays only 2.30–5.30pm) documents the unfortunate episode in its local history exhibition.

Triora is a pretty village. Cobbled alleyways lead through a labyrinth of picturesque houses, many of which now stand empty because the inhabitants have moved to the big city. Today Triora has a population of just 300; 40 years ago it was four times that number, and during the Late Middle Ages, when there was an important connecting route between the sea, Brigue and Tende, 500 families lived here. The village contains the ruins of five fortresses and castles, three of the original seven town gates and almost a dozen churches and chapels. The Romanesque-Gothic **Santa Maria Assunta** contains a painting by Luca Cambiaso and also an altar panel of *The Baptism of Christ* by Taddeo de Bartolo from 1397 – thought to be the oldest painting in Western Liguria.

Taggia facades

Taggia: Via San Dalmazzo

Travel via the seaside resort of Arma di Taggia now to reach the culturally important town of ★★ **Taggia**. According to legend, Benedictine monks from Piedmont converted the local population during the 7th century – not only to Christianity but also to olive cultivation. Olives, citrus fruits, almonds and figs all took the place of the town's former traditional dairy farming and maritime pursuits, and very soon brought the town prosperity. Today the churches, magnificent town houses and noble portals all testify to the town's former greatness. The most attractive of these palazzi can be seen in the Via Curlo, the Via Gastaldi, the **Via San Dalmazzo** and the arcaded Via Soleri, in which a picturesque antiques market is held every month. Biblical symbols and the coats-of-arms of noble

...amilies can still be seen in the reliefs on the slate portals; the Napoleonic revolutionary troops vented their anger on the nobility here in 1797. The originally medieval bridge across the Argentina river has 16 arches and is 260m (850ft) long; the river itself is usually nothing more than a stream, but becomes a torrent after heavy rainfall. In the upper part of town, the Romanesque church of **Madonna del Canneto** has a 12th-century crypt and also several fine 16th-century frescoes by Giovanni and Luca Cambiaso and also Francesco Brea, a nephew of the more famous Ludovico Brea.

Catching up on the gossip

Many of the works of this celebrated artist can be admired inside the ★★ **Dominican monastery**, just outside Taggia's town gates. The monastery church alone contains five valuable altar paintings by Ludovico Brea, who was born in Nice in 1450 and died in Genoa in 1523. The Dominicans had arrived here in Taggia in 1468, and between 1483 and 1513 Brea produced his altar paintings *St Catherine of Siena*, the *Baptism of Christ* and the *Annunciation*, all of them set against Gothic gold backgrounds. During a visit to Lombardy, Brea came in contact with the new Renaissance style, and its influence is clear in his *Madonna of the Rosary* where the gold background has suddenly been replaced by a realistic landscape reminiscent of Leonardo. The earlier Piedmontese artist Giovanni Canavesio, active on the Western Riviera and in the Nice region between 1472 and 1500, did the altar painting of *St Dominic*, also owned by the church. More works by Canavesio, Ludovico Brea and his nephew Francesco Brea can be admired in the chapter house and also in the monastery's small museum (daily except Thursday 9.30am–noon and 3–5pm), open to visitors on request.

Dominican detail

63

From old-fashioned art to modern art now: a road leads from Arma di Taggia up to the village of ★ **Bussana-Vecchia**, where a colony of artists and craftsmen has lived since the 1960s. This magnificently situated village was destroyed by an earthquake in 1887, and while the new town of Bussana was being built at a different site down by the sea, the mountain village of Bussana Vecchia fell into decay. The houses and walls collapsed and became overgrown. During the 1950s several families from Southern Italy who had come to Liguria to work in the flower industry tried briefly to resurrect Bussana Vecchia from the dead, but were soon forced to abandon the idea. In 1963 a group of artists made a renewed attempt: despite fierce protests from the municipality of San Remo, to which the village belongs, they began repairing and restoring the less damaged buildings, and opened several studios and workshops. This former ghost town has now become an international artists' colony.

Art at Bussana-Vecchia

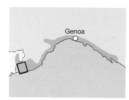

Route 7

The Cosmopolitan and the Traditional

San Remo – Ceriana – Baiardo – Apricale – Dolceac-qua – Bordighera (50km/30 miles) *See map p58*

It was during the 19th century that English lords, Russian tsars and German emperors began spending their winters on the Riviera – tourism was born. The villas, art nouveau hotels and palm-lined sea promenades of San Remo and Bordighera still have a very elegant, cosmopolitan flair of their own. The atmosphere up in the mountain villages, reached from the coast via steep winding roads, is quite different. Peace and quiet reigns, the mountain panoramas are breathtaking, and many of the traditional customs, such as the Festa della Barca in Baiardo, date back to pagan times. As a defence measure against the Saracens, several distinctly labyrinthine towns were built in this region over the centuries, one such being the highly atmospheric Dolceacqua.

Allow a day for this route – it'll leave time for a stroll or two through the tiny villages up in the mountains.

San Remo

It's surprising that ★ **San Remo** still hasn't built any kind of monument to the Italian writer Giovanni Ruffini (1807–81). He wasn't one of the greatest names in Italian literature, but he still laid the foundation for the success of the Italian Riviera. His rather kitschy novel *Doctor Antonio*, which he wrote in English and had published in Edinburgh in 1855, is set in San Remo and Bordighera. It was a great success, and several of its readers decided to go and see the Ligurian coast for themselves. The first guests who came to enjoy the mild climate of the Riviera were housed in a private villa belonging to Countess Adele Roverizio di Roccasterone. The Grand Hotel Londra was built in 1860, soon followed by the Royal, still the most exclusive hotel in town today. By the turn of the 20th century there were 25 hotels and around 200 villas; travellers today have a choice of around 250 hotels, campsites and holiday villages, all of differing standards.

Although San Remo became a popular destination for modern tourism after World War II it still likes to remember the good old days when emperors, empresses, tsars and tsarinas all came here, along with princes, dukes, writers and famous artists. The town today has a population of 56,000, and is equipped with the very latest facilities for golf, riding, tennis, sailing, windsurfing and water-skiing; car rallies and sailing regattas of international renown are also held here regularly. All that remains of the *belle époque* these days is the appearance of the

Villa Nobel

place: the grand hotels with their wedding-cake facades, the Corso Imperatrice with its statue of *Spring* draped with garlands, and the elegant villas. The art nouveau movement has left several impressive traces in San Remo, including the **Villa Nobel**, where Alfred Nobel spent the final years of his life (1891–96). Today it is the seat of the International Institute of Human Rights. Another grand building dating from the turn of the century is of course the **Casino Municipale**. Designed by the French architect Eugène Ferret and built between 1904 and 1906, it earns San Remo millions. Rumours have been circulating recently that the casino is being used by the mafia and the *camorra* to launder money, but that hasn't diminished the fascination of such games as *Chemin de fer*, roulette and blackjack for its regular clientele.

65

Casino Municipale

The name San Remo is synonymous with all that is cosmopolitan. In fact the town should really be known as San Romolo – the name of a small village up in the mountains slightly inland. The Ligurians who lived here before the Romans came built several forts up on the hilltops around San Remo during the 6th and 5th centuries BC, and when the Romans first reached the Riviera in the 2nd century BC they founded the town of *Villa Matutiana*, later converted to Christianity by the Genoese bishop Romolo in the 8th century AD. San Romolo then gradually became San Römu.

Marking the beginning of the Corso Imperatrice is the Russian Orthodox church of **San Basilio** (Tuesday, Thursday and Saturday 3–6.30pm, Sunday 9.30am–12.30pm and 3–6.30pm), the construction of which was financed by the Russian 'colony' here during the late 19th century. The large 16th-century Palazzo Borea d'Olmo not only contains a gallery of local art but also the **Civico Museo Archeologico** (Tuesday to Saturday 9am–noon and 3–6.30pm), Sunday 9am–noon, closed Monday), with

Church of San Basilio

Exploring La Pigna

Ceriana

its prehistoric collection of finds from the Stone, Bronze and Iron Ages, along with some Roman remains.

The facade of the Late Romanesque cathedral of **San Siro**, built in the 13th century above the ruins of a former church on the site, was completely renovated in around 1900. Opposite the left-hand portal with its bas-reliefs is the Battistero, originally a Roman three-aisled church before it was turned into a centralised structure during the 17th century.

Those planning to stay the night in San Remo should try to get up early and visit one of the daily flower auctions, which start at 5am in the **Mercato dei Fiori**. San Remo is the largest flower centre in Italy – the greenhouses stretch along the Western Riviera for miles.

San Remo has another side, however: the old town of **La Pigna** further uphill, all of it far less elegant and actually rather dilapidated. The picturesque jumble of narrow alleyways, flights of steps, vaulted passageways and buttressed houses is mainly inhabited today by the old and the poor of San Remo, Southern Italians working in the flower trade, and also North African immigrants still waiting to be integrated. The old town is dominated by the richly-decorated baroque pilgrimage church of **Madonna della Costa** (17th-century); there's a good view of the gulf and the town from the square in front of it.

The old part of San Remo has been neglected for half a century; local critics regularly complain that similar places in Provence have all been turned into picturesque tourist villages by now. Today San Remo is turning into one giant old people's home: one third of the population is over 60 years of age, and wealthy pensioners from the neighbouring regions are gradually transforming the town into an Italian version of Florida. In addition there has been a recent influx of very rich Russians, in true pre-revolutionary tradition, many of whom have moved into the most expensive and exclusive hotels in town.

After a detour to the **Pinacoteca Rambaldi** (Wednesday, Friday and Sunday 9am–noon, Wednesday, Thursday and Saturday 3–6pm) in Coldiroldi, which contains a rather haphazardly arranged collection of paintings from the 15th to the 19th centuries, and also a valuable library, the route continues out of San Remo and through several well-preserved mountain villages which illustrate Liguria's 'other' face very successfully. The first stop on the route is the medieval village of **Ceriana**, distinctive for the way in which its streets are laid out: they follow the natural contours of the steep slope. The village is dominated by the twin-towered parish church of **San Pietro e Paolo**, with its baroque facade; inside there is a polyptych by an anonymous 16th-century artist and a triptych by Francesco Brea

Baiardo

dating from 1545. The Romanesque church of Sant'Andrea, with its distinctive spire, contains four Doric columns originally taken from a pagan temple.

In the mountain village of ★ **Baiardo** (900m/2,950ft above sea level), which has largely retained its original character, the locals celebrate the Festa della Barca every Whit Sunday. *Barca* is the Italian word for ship, and the ceremony may date back to pagan times. A tall pole of pine resembling a ship's mast is erected in the square outside the church and decorated with lots of greenery; then a group of folk dancers circle it very slowly, singing a sad song about a lord of Baiardo's daughter who fell in love with a ship's captain.

One real tragedy for Baiardo was the severe earthquake of 23 February 1887, when the roof of the church of **San Nicolò** collapsed and over 200 people died. The effects of that tremor can still be observed today in the upper part of the village, where the church ruins bear testimony to the incredible power of the quake. The putti-adorned altar of St Anthony among the ruined walls is a moving sight; mass is still celebrated in front of it.

The church of San Nicolò

Experienced hikers should definitely ascend the **Monte Bignone** (1,299m/4,260ft) behind San Remo; the trip takes 4½ hours, and the view from the top in good weather is quite breathtaking.

Domestic architecture

A few miles further along one of those narrow panoramic roads, so typical of the Ligurian hinterland, and **Apricale** comes into view. At the entrance to it there are Gothic gates dating from the 13th century, but Apricale – like many other Ligurian villages these days – is gradually growing depopulated. The main square is especially picturesque, with the parish church Purificazione di Maria, rebuilt in the 19th and 20th centuries, and opposite it the Oratorio di San Bartolomeo with its rococo stucco dec-

Apricale: the main square

oration. The Palazzo del Comune also lies on this piazza; like the other buildings it, too, has contemporary murals depicting rural life and Ligurian landscapes. Beyond the former defensive wall is the fortress-like, late medieval church of **Santa Maria degli Angeli**, with its single-aisled interior full of newly-restored fresco cycles dating from the 15th and 18th centuries; the ones depicting the *Assumption* and the *Evangelists* are probably among the oldest. The cemetery church of Sant'Antonio Abate has undergone alteration over the centuries, but still retains a simple Romanesque apse.

A detour to **Perinaldo** is also a detour away from the remote Ligurian mountains into the world of international science. Giovanni Domenico Cassini was born here in 1625, the first in a long line of astronomers and mathematicians who ran the Paris Observatory for several generations. Cassini's nephew Giacomo Filippo Maraldi was no less illustrious; also born in Perinaldo, in 1665, he held a top post at the court of Louis XIV, the 'Sun King'. Little wonder that the main street of this long-drawn-out village is named after him and a local restaurant is called 'Pianeti di Giove' ('Planets of Jupiter'). The placement of the church of **Santuario della Vistiazione** just outside the village is worthy of note: on Cassini's initiative it was aligned with the 'Ligurian line of longitude', and therefore throws no shadow at all on 21 June each year.

After a series of dizzying mountain hairpins, the route reaches **Isolabona** down in the valley once more – the Val Nervia, filled with vineyards and olive groves. Instead of driving straight back towards the coast, however, it's well worth heading back into the mountains at this point. Pass the pilgrimage church of **Nostra Signora delle Grazie**, with its unusual 16th-century painting of the family tree of Jesse, and soon the rather unremarkable-looking but culturally very interesting village of **Pigna** comes into view. During medieval times Pigna used to be situated down in the valley, but was soon shifted to the hillside above for strategic reasons. The facade of the 15th-century parish church of San Michele is adorned by a magnificent marble rose window, the first ever produced by the Lombard sculptor Giovanni Gagini, many of whose important works can be admired in Genoa. The polyptych inside depicting St Michael is a mature work by the Piedmontese painter Giovanni Canavesio (ca 1500), who also executed the rather grotesque-looking frescoes in the cemetery church of San Bernardino.

Making a point in Pigna

A much-photographed humpbacked bridge, which fascinated the artist Claude Monet over 100 years ago, con-

nects the two sections of ★★**Dolceacqua**. The medieval part, called Terra, makes it clear how Ligurian villages defended themselves against enemy attack at that time: only the locals knew their way through the labyrinth of buildings and passageways, many of which could be bolted shut. Above the town is a ruined Doria **fortress** in which cultural events are held during the summer months (daily except Tuesday 9am–noon and 3–7pm). A modern monument in front of the baroque parish church of **Sant'Antonio** commemorates a local hero, Pier Vincenzo Mela; during the 18th century he discovered how the remains of pressed olives could be turned into oil. The oil sold in Dolceacqua comes from the very best, hand-selected olives, and meals are best accompanied by the delicious local red known as *Rossese di Dolceacqua*, the third wine in Liguria alongside *Cinque Terre* and *Colli di Luni* to have received the coveted DOC qualification.

Dolceacqua's humpback bridge and parish church

The route now continues via Camporosso back along the coast as far as ★**Bordighera**. Like San Remo, this town has two sections, both very different from each other: the old town, huddled up on the Capo Sant'Ampelio, once owned by fishermen and farmers, with its excellent view across the coast from the Spianata del Capo; and down in the plain, the elegant, noble, 'garden-city' section, which has given itself up completely to tourism. The 19th-century Municipio was designed by Charles Garnier, who also built the Paris Opera House. Bordighera was another popular summer spa resort with the English, and perhaps the most famous member of the town's English colony was the botanist Clarence Bicknell, who was also an Anglican clergyman here. He not only founded the international municipal library but also the **Museo Bicknell** (Monday to Friday 9am–1pm and 3–6pm), which contains several fascinating exhibits including thousands of prints of the prehistoric cave drawings from Mont Bégo (*see page 73*).

Ventimiglia rooftops

Ventimiglia alleys

Route 8

Prehistoric Liguria

Ventimiglia – Tenda (50km/31 miles) *See map p58*

This route leads across to France's Val de Tende, just next to Liguria, and there are traces of the region's earliest settlers on either side of the border. The mild Riviera climate was already being enjoyed 200,000 years ago in the caves of the Balzi Rossi near Ventimiglia, and between 4,000 and 6,000 years ago people immortalised their daily life and their faith in a series of 45,000 rock drawings in the Vallée des Merveilles, near the French town of Tende.

A trip back into the distant past needs peace and quiet, so it's best to allow a full day for this route.

Most visitors to **Ventimiglia** spend only very little time there, treating it as a rather chaotic border town that's only worth visiting for its weekly market each Friday. This doesn't do it justice, however: the old town with its jumble of ancient houses to the west of the Roia, and also the newer section to the east of the river contain a number of interesting sights, as well as remains of the old Roman town.

Ventimiglia's rather gloomy Old Town with its tall, dark houses and washing hung out to dry on endless lines is more reminiscent of Southern Italy than the Riviera. It's in these streets, however, that Ventimiglia's most interesting sights can be found. The ★ **cathedral of Santa Maria Assunta**, for instance, with its crypt full of pre-Romanesque sculpture, or the octagonal baptistery next to it and the church of **San Michele**, both of which date back to the 11th century; over the centuries they have received various alterations and additions.

San Michele

Genoa

To the east of Ventimiglia is the archaeological site known as **Area Archeologica di Albintimilium**, containing the remains of what was once a flourishing Roman community 2,000 years ago. The trapezoid town wall and three town gates dating from around 50BC can still be clearly made out, as can the baths built during the reign of Augustus, and also an amphitheatre from the 2nd century AD with a seating capacity of 5,000. When it came to strategically important towns, the Romans were always generous with their municipal architecture: the town of *Albintimilium* lay on the trading route to Gaul and Spain, and also on the *Via Julia Augusta*. Several fascinating finds dating from Roman times are on display in the **Museo Civico Archeologico** (daily except Monday 9.30am–noon and 3–5pm, July to September 5–7pm).

Go much further back into the past now, however, with a visit to the ★ **Balzi Rossi Caves**, situated at the foot of some red cliffs in Grimaldi, just next to the Franco-Italian border. Excavation work began here in the middle of the 19th century, and towards the end of it Prince Albert I of Monaco decided to finance exploration of a cave named after him, the Grotta del Principe. The skeleton of *Arconthropus* man that was discovered here is thought to be around 200,000 years old.

Three far younger skeletons, of Cro Magnon men (15,000–30,000 years old), were discovered in the Barma Grande Cave; and the necklaces of sea-shells found in the Grotta dei Fanciulli are highly artistic. The **Museo Preistorico dei Balzi Rossi** (daily 9am–7pm, caves open until 1 hour before sunset) documents the various fascinating finds from these caves, which are situated right next to the sea.

The Balzi Rossi Museum was founded in 1898 by Thomas Hanbury, a successful British merchant, who is even more famous on the Riviera for his ★ **Giardino Hanbury** (June to September daily 9am–6pm, October to May daily except Wednesday 10am–5pm). When he first came here in 1867 to recover from bronchitis he fell in love with Cape Mortola near Ventimiglia, with its bougainvillea, Aleppo pine, olive and lemon trees, and promptly bought it. He then laid out a botanical garden suitable for exotic plants. At first he was helped by his brother Daniel, an experienced botanist.

The gardens slope down towards the sea on a southern slope sheltered from the wind, and cover a vast area. Over 4,000 different species of plant from five continents grow here, and 3km (2 miles) of paths, intersecting at the lower end of the gardens with the old Roman *Via Julia Augusta*, lead past palms and agaves, banana and bamboo, Japanese gardens, fruit groves and Australian bush. The Hanbury Gardens are maintained by experts from the

71

Hanbury Gardens

Contrasts in Airole

This way to France

Gorges de Saorge

University of Genoa, and a small garden café with a fine view of the coast rounds off any visit here magnificently.

The Val Roia begins in Ventimiglia, and despite the fact that it crosses almost 40km (24 miles) of French territory it's still the best way from Western Liguria to Cuneo and Turin in Piedmont. During the Middle Ages the old salt route led through this valley, connecting the salt-pans in Nice with the Lombardy plain. To begin with, the villages here are very similar to others in the Ligurian hinterland: the stone houses are all huddled together, and the slopes are covered with ancient, silvery olive-groves. In **Airole** the grey of the houses contrasts pleasantly with the bright-yellow stuccoed facade of the baroque parish church of Santi Filippi e Giacomo, built during the 17th century.

The picturesque and atmospheric hamlet of Fanghetto, right on the French border, with its Romanesque bridge, is actually a part of the village of **San Michele**. The landscape starts getting drier and more alpine now: the olive groves are now replaced by forests of larch and pine, and the first large community on French soil is **Breil-sur-Roya** on the left bank of the river.

The adventurously narrow ravine known as the **Gorges de Saorge** has just enough room for one road and a small stream, and at the end of it there's a fascinating view of the magnificently situated mountain village of **Saorge**, high up on the steep slope. A hike at this point (approx 3 hours) along a much-travelled medieval connecting route between Saorge and the Ligurian village of Pigna (*see Route 7, page 68*), leads up to the 1,161-m (3,800-ft) high Passo Muratone. At the top of the pass the tour along the Franco-Italian border ridge can be extended still further to include the Toraggio-Pietravecchia Massif, with its many caves and the dizzying Sentiero degli Alpini (*see Route 6, page 61*).

The route then leads through the Gorges de Bergue, another ravine with brown-and-green slate walls, to reach **Saint-Dalmas-de-Tende**. Devotees of ecclesiastical art will definitely head straight for the medieval village of **La Brigue** at this point and visit the pilgrimage church of ★ **Notre-Dame-des-Fontaines**, towering above a romantic gorge. The church, which was first mentioned in 1375 and is rather inconspicuous from the outside, contains an artistic treasure unique in all the Alps. The Piedmontese painter Giovanni Canavesio, whose work we already admired in Taggia (*see Route 6, page 62*) and Pigna (*see Route 7, page 68*), painted the interior of this church with several magnificent ★★ **fresco cycles**. A full 320sq m (3,500sq ft) are covered with highly impressive paintings on religious themes including the *Last Judgement*, the *Passion of Christ* and the *Life of the Virgin*, and in all of them Canavesio adds a realistic, mocking touch of his own. Oddly enough the fresco cycle was completed on 12 October 1492 – the same day on which Christopher Columbus discovered America.

Not far away from the church, to the west of Saint-Dalmas-de-Tende, is a prehistoric cult site. The 2,872-m (9,420-ft) high **Mont Bégo** was considered sacred by Liguria's earliest inhabitants, and the Vallée des Merveilles along its southwestern flank contains around 45,000 ★★ **rock drawings**. Most of them date from the Bronze Age (1800–1500BC), and portray weapons, farmers with ploughs, huts, fields, geometrical figures and also a large number of animals with horns, indicating some kind of ancient fertility cult. In the summer months shepherds still come up here from the Ligurian coast and from Provence with their flocks and herds, and it was probably their forefathers who drew the sharply stylised figures on the smooth rock-faces in the region. Much of this primitive art is catalogued in the remarkable prehistoric museum opened in the 19th century by Clarence Bicknell (*see page 69*); from 1881 onwards he used to spend many summers up here in a house he built himself in Casterino, on the northwestern slope of Mont Bégo. The region containing the rock drawings has been part of the French national park of Percantour since 1979, and has been classified as a natural site of international importance by UNESCO. Because of vandalism, however, several of the prehistoric drawings can now only be visited in the company of a guide.

From the Lac des Mesces (1,375m/4,500ft above sea level) which can be reached by car from Saint-Dalmas-de-Tende, the **Vallée des Merveilles** is another 2½ hours on foot. The valley is open – weather permitting – from June to mid-October. The most famous drawing in this 'valley of miracles' is the so-called *Chef de Tribu* ('tribal chieftain'), and unlike many others it can be touched – because it's a copy, and the original is safe and well in the museum in Tende.

Tende is an old and picturesque trading town, dominated by the ruins of a medieval castle destroyed by French troops in 1691. Many of the houses in the centre have sculpted portals with inscriptions dating from the 15th and 16th centuries. The main portal of the cathedral of **Notre-Dame de l'Assomption**, which was consecrated in 1518, is particularly fine. Masons from the Ligurian village of Cenova cut these reliefs of the *Assumption*, the *Annunciation* and *Christ with the Twelve Apostles* from greenish-grey serpentine – a good example of the kind of 'cultural exchange' that has been going on between the Italians and the French in this border region for centuries.

Notre-Dame-des-Fontaines

73

Tende cathedral

Art History

It's true that Liguria isn't one of the most famous cultural areas of Italy, but even here a trip to the beach can easily be combined with a visit to a museum, a church, a historic palazzo, or a theatre or music festival.

Early settlement

The oldest artefacts in Liguria (5,000–6,000 years old) are the cave paintings on Mont Bégo (*see page 73*). They aren't that easy to reach, however: the caves lie on French territory and are at the end of a mountain hike lasting several hours. The mysterious stelae from Lunigiana, not far from Liguria, date from the Bronze Age and can be admired in La Spezia's museum.

Stelae from Lunigiana

Roman remains

The old Roman road from Albenga to Alassio is a monument to Roman civil engineering. There are also five Roman bridges in the Val Ponci near Finale, and the ruins of some Roman villas in Bussana and San Remo. The best preserved structure dating from antiquity, however, is in Ventimiglia: the Roman *Albintimilium*. Luni also has a forum, a temple of Diana, and the villas Casa dei Mosaici and Casa degli Affreschi, all of them bearing testimony to the former might of the Romans' 'marble harbour'; cultural events are still staged in the amphitheatre today.

75

Medieval

The list of places with medieval art and architecture is endless. The most important works which no visitor to Liguria should miss include the Early Christian baptistery and cathedral in Albenga, the Basilica dei Fieschi in Lavagna and the Abbazia di Borzone inland from it, the baptistery and church of San Michele in Ventimiglia, the monasteries of San Domenico in Taggia and San Fruttuoso di Capodimonte near Portofino, as well as the churches of San Paragorio in Noli and San Pietro in Portovenere.

Albenga cathedral

Gothic to Renaissance

During the 15th century the Dominican monastery in Taggia became a bastion of Gothic painting, and there are several Renaissance features too; the two main artists involved here were Giovanni Canavesio and Ludovico Brea. Around the same time, stonemasons provided countless palazzi and churches with magnificently carved Gothic slate portals; there's hardly a town or village without one.

The rather provincial history of art in Liguria was brightened up a lot by the Florentine painter Perin del Vaga, who provided Genoa's Palazzo Doria with its magnificent frescoes; his successor Luca Cambiaso (1527–85) influ-

Palazzo Reale in Genoa

enced whole generations of 17th- and 18th-century artists including Bernardo Strozzi, Domenico Piola, Bernardo Castello, and Gregorio and Lorenzo De Ferrari.

Renaissance Villas

The exceptionally mild climate of Genoa and its environs encouraged wealthy families to build splendid villas in or near the city. When these private villas became public property, they were a real discovery, not least because many of them are surrounded by magnificent parks and gardens. It was back in the mid-16th century that Galeazzo Alessi, an Umbrian-born architect trained in Rome, arrived in Genoa and with his Renaissance Villa Giustiani-Cambiaso provided the basis for countless more town palazzi and country villas that were built during the two centuries that followed, including the splendid Villa Serra in Sant'Ilario, surrounded by one of the most picturesque parks in all Italy and the famous Villa Gropallo in Nervi. The Villa Durazzo Pallavicini in the west of Genoa, enlivened by outbuildings and fountains, is described as the pearl among the villas of Liguria.

Art nouveau in San Remo

Later developments

A new construction boom began in the second half of the 19th century when the Riviera was discovered by foreign tourists and many neoclassical buildings appeared. Many of these can be seen along the Western Riviera (note the buildings by Charles Garnier in Bordighera) and were influenced by the art nouveau movement. The railway station in Savona was designed in 1960 by one of the most gifted architects in Italy at present, Pier Luigi Nervi.

Festival Calendar

January   **20** Festival of St Sebastian in Dolceacqua and Camporosso; a decorated laurel tree is carried through the town.

Easter   Processions held in Ceriana on Maundy Thursday and Good Friday, and in Savona and Triora on Good Friday.

May   **First Sunday** the *sagro del pesce* in Camogli; vast amounts of fish are fried in an enormous frying pan and distributed among guests for free.

Whit Sunday   *Festa della barca*; ritual dance around a tree-trunk, dating back to pagan fertility rituals.

Sunday after Corpus Christi   *Infiorata* in Diano Marina and Sassello; the streets are strewn with flowers.

Festival time in Diano Marina

June   **24** Festival of St John; solemn procession to celebrate the patron saint.

July   **1–3** *Nostra Signora di Montallegro* in Rapallo; procession and firework display at the popular pilgrimage church.

August   **First Sunday** *Stella Maris* in Camogli; atmospheric boat procession.
Palio del Golfo in La Spezia. Festival on the water with regatta and fireworks.
Corteo Storico in Ventimiglia; procession in period costumes to commemorate a historical event.

Fireworks in La Spezia

August   **13–14** *Torta dei Fieschi* in Lavagna; festival commemorating medieval *fieschi* weddings, with a giant cake, tournaments and a historical procession.

August   **23** *Cristo degli Abissi* in San Fruttuoso; divers descend to a bronze statue of Christ lying on the ocean floor.

September   **Second Sunday** *Regata dei Rioni* in Noli; regatta with historical procession.

December   **13** *Santa Lucia* in Tiorano; festival with a torchlight procession.

Food and Drink

Ligurian cooking is country cooking. The numerous Riviera restaurants with their very varied seafood and sauces do little to change this fact. Despite their seafaring past and more than 300km (180 miles) of coastline, the Ligurians are essentially a traditional farming people, and genuine Ligurian cuisine is influenced markedly by local agricultural produce.

The main ingredient of *Trenette con pesto*, the Ligurians' favourite dish, is basil, an aromatic herb which has long been a staple of local cuisine (it was taken on long sea journeys by mariners through the centuries as protection against scurvy and similar diseases). The *pesto* sauce also contains grated cheese, a lot of garlic and pure olive oil, and is then poured over flat noodles. This sauce is also served with lasagne in Liguria. *Ceci* are another very important ingredient in local cooking. These are small, yellow chick-peas, which originally came from the Orient, and they provide the basis for the two vegetable soups known as *Mesciua* and *Zimino di ceci*, as well as for two classics of Ligurian cuisine, the *Panissa* and the *Farinata*. A *Panissa* is a kind of chick-pea paste cut into slices and then fried in oil, and the *Farinata* is a thin pancake made of chick-pea flour which can be sampled at traditional 'Farinotti' establishments. Another very typical dish is the *Focaccia*, a pancake made of dough that is sprinkled with oil and then baked.

Restaurant in Pieve di Teco

79

Popular main courses include salted quiches, the most famous of which is the multi-layered *Torta pasqualina*, with vegetables, eggs and other ingredients. Ligurian housewives and cooks pride themselves on cooking vegetables stuffed with various (vegetarian) ingredients, such as onions, aubergines, tomatoes or peppers. Creating a *cappon magro* requires a great deal of time and patience: it is a pyramid consisting of six or seven different kinds of cooked fish with lots of different vegetables, and is decorated with shrimps, oysters and other crustaceans. The dish is served in restaurants but always has to be ordered in advance. As far as meat is concerned, chicken and rabbit dishes tend to predominate; the seafood dishes very often feature sardines (stuffed, of course) and stockfish. The main reason why Ligurian cuisine is so delicious is the subtle mixture of fresh herbs employed – especially marjoram, oregano and basil – that is very reminiscent of nearby Provence.

Fresh catch

Great coffee

A good meal deserves a good wine, and there's no shortage of those. So far, the DOC label has been earned by just three of the local wines: the white, delicate *Cinque Terre*, the rich red wine called *Rossese di Dolceacqua* and the lighter, fruitier red known as *Colli di Luni*.

Restaurants

The following selection, from the region's most popular destinations, are listed according to three categories: $$$ = expensive, $$ = medium-priced and $ = inexpensive.

Alassio
$$$Palma, Via Cavour 5, tel: 0182-640 314. Provençal-style food. **$$La Vigna**, Via Lepanto Solva 1, tel: 0182-643 301. Nice location, rustic atmosphere, traditional dishes.

Albisola Marina
$$$Gianni ai Pescatori, Corso Bigliati 82, tel: 019-481 200. Ligurian seafood, Tuscan wines and a stylish atmosphere. **$$La Familiare**, Piazza del Popolo 8, tel: 019-489 480. Genuine Ligurian cooking.

Ameglia
$$$Paracucchi-Locanda dell'Angelo, Viale XXV Aprile 60, Ameglia. A restaurant attached to a hotel and considered *the* best place to eat in all of Italy. **$$Dai Pironcelli**, Montemarcello, Via della Mura 45, tel: 0187-601 252. Local fish and meat dishes, charming and efficient service.

Arma di Taggia
$$$La Conchiglia, Via Lungomare 33, tel: 0184-43169. Old fishermen's house by the sea, charming atmosphere, Ligurian cuisine.

Borgio Verezzi
$$Da Caxetta, Piazza San Pietro, tel: 019-610 106. Genuine Ligurian cuisine under an ancient vaulted ceiling. **$$Antica Osteria Saracena del Bergallo**, Via Roma 17, tel: 019-610 487. Local specialities and a great view.

Camogli
$$Vento Ariel, Calata Porto, tel: 0185-771 080. Excellent seafood, good view of harbour. **$$Spadin**, tel: 0185-770 624. Romantically situated on the Punta Chiappa, only accessible by boat or on foot.

Camporosso
$$La Via Romana, Via Romana 57, tel: 0184-266 681. Art nouveau atmosphere in luxury hotel, and suitably delicious food. **$$Mistral**, Via Aurelia 23, tel: 0184-262 306. Seafood and vegetables with a Provençal touch.

Ceriana
$Fontana Bianca, Valle Armea Nord, tel: 0184-551 079. Nice trattoria with tasty and varied dishes.

Cinque Terre

$$$Gambero Rosso, Vernazza, Piazza Marconi 7, tel: 0187-812 265. Classic establishment with good food and great atmosphere. **$$Da Peo**, Monterosso al Mare, Via XX Settembre 32, tel: 0187-818 384. All kinds of fish dishes served within medieval walls. **$$De Manan**, Corniglia, Via Fieschi 117, tel: 0187-821 166. Bucolic Osteria in 14th-century building, good seafood.

Dolceacqua

$Gastone, Piazza Garibaldi, tel: 0184-206 577. Near the castle, serves rabbit and lamb dishes as well as seafood.

Finalborgo

$$Torchi, Via dell'Annunziata, tel: 019-690 531. Elegance and good food in a former 16th-century oil-mill.

Genoa

$$$Antica Osteria del Bai, Via Quarto 12, tel: 010-387 478. Inconspicuous from the outside but a real gourmet paradise within. **$$Trattoria da Rina**, Via Mura delle Grazie 3r, tel: 010-246 6475. Nice fish restaurant near the harbour. **$Ferrando**, Via Carli 110, tel: 010-751 925. Nice establishment up in the hills behind the city, with interesting herbal additions to its delicious food. **$Da Maria**, Vico Testadoro 14r, tel: 010-581 080. Genuine Genoese cuisine right in the heart of the old town. **$Sa Pesta**, Via dei Giustiniani 16r, tel: 010-208 636. Good traditional dishes.

Grimaldi

$$Baia Beniamin, Grimaldi Inferiore, Corso Europa 63, tel: 0184-38002. A feast for the eyes, and what's more it even tastes fantastic.

Genoa bar

81

Al fresco in Portofino

Shade in Pigna
La Spezia market

La Spezia
$Il Moccia, Pegazzano, Via Chiesa 30, tel: 0187-707 029. Nice trattoria serving genuine Ligurian fare.

Lavagna
$$L'Armia, Corso Garibaldi 68, tel: 0185-305 441. Good Ligurian fare. **$Luchin**, Via Bighetti 51-53, tel: 0185-301 063. Trattoria in the medieval old town.

Pigna
$La Posta, Via San Rocco 60, tel: 0184-241 666. Home cooking, delicious, best at weekends. **Osteria del Portico**, Castel Vittorio, Via Umberto 16, tel: 0184-241 352. Simple restaurant with traditional and delicious food.

Porto Maurizio
$$Convivium, Via Vecchie Carceri 19, tel: 0183-61780. Local specialities. **$$Osteria dell'Olio Grosso**, Piazza Parasio 36, tel: 0183-60815. Good seafood restaurant in the old town.

Portofino

Portofino
$$$Il Pitosforo, Molo Umberto 19, tel: 0185-269 020. A Portofino institution, right beside the harbour and very expensive.

Portovenere
$$Taverna del Corsaro, Calata Doria 102, tel: 0187-790 622. Excellent seafood. **$Antica Osteria del Carrugio**, Via Cappellini 66, tel: 0187-790 617. Nice old restaurant in town centre. **$$Locanda Lorena**, Palmaria Island, tel: 0187-902 370. Magnificent viewing terrace to eat outside, and eight rooms for a relaxing stay.

Rapallo
$$U Giancu, San Massimo, tel: 0185-260 505. Lots of original cartoons round the walls and (almost) vegetarian cooking.

Recco
$$Manuelina, Via Roma 228, tel: 0185-75364. Delicious Ligurian specialities.

San Ludovico
$$$Balzi Rossi, Ponte San Ludovico, tel: 0184-38132. Magnificently situated, excellent food, regularly attracts French people from across the border. **$$Marco Polo**, Lungomare Cavalotti, tel: 0184-352 678. Right next to the sea, good Ligurian specialities.

San Remo
$$$Paolo e Barbara, Via Roma 47, tel: 0184-531 653. Exclusive and highly imaginative food. **$$Il Bagatto**, Corso Mateotti 145, tel: 0184-531 925. Nouvelle cuisine served up in the old palazzo of the dukes of Borea d'Olmo. **$Bacchus**, Via Roma 65, tel: 0184-530 990. Elegant atmosphere balanced by substantial Ligurian food. **$Le Cantine Sanremesi**, Via Palazzo 7, tel: 0184-572 063. Centrally located wine cellar with a good choice of typical dishes and snacks.

Santa Margherita Ligure
$$Il Frantoio, Via Giuncheto 23a, tel: 0185-286 667. Excellent food, inside the former oil-mill of the Villa Durazzo, pizzas also available.

Sarzana
$Il Cantinone, Via Fiasella, tel: 0187-627 952. Traditional cuisine served in a former wine cellar.

Savona
$$Osteria Bacco, Via Guarda Superiore 17r, tel: 019-833 5350. Distinctive establishment at the harbour, excellent Ligurian cuisine, all at very decent prices. **$$Antica Osteria Bosco delle Ninfe**, Via Ranco 10, tel: 019-823 976. Good views, good food.

Sestri Levante
$$Flammenghilla Fieschi, Via Pestella 6 (Trigoso 4km/2½ miles), tel: 0185-481 041. Stylish restaurant inside an old Fieschi villa. **$$Polpo Mario**, Via XXV Aprile 163, tel: 0185-480 203. Classic, but imaginative cooking. **$Bottega del Vino**, Via Nazionale 530, tel: 0185-43349. Attractive and popular wine bar with a good selection of local wines, as well as tasty snacks.

Rapallo

Cooling fruit

Scenic Sestri Levante

Active Holidays

The Riviera is a paradise for swimmers and mountain climbers alike. There's a vast range of activities on offer for the actively inclined.

Golf

There are five idyllically situated golf courses in Liguria. Two 9-hole courses are located in Arenzano, in the province of Genoa, and in Marigola near Lerici (province of La Spezia); the three 18-hole courses are at Garlenda (province of Savona), Rapallo (province of Genoa) and San Remo (province of Imperia). For more information contact the Federazione Italiana Golf (FIG), Comitato Regionale Liguria, Piazza Rossetti 5/9, I-16129 Genoa, tel: 010-592410.

Hiking and mountain-climbing

Into the mountains

The Italians themselves are growing increasingly interested in hiking, and many new routes are now being opened in the Ligurian Alps and Ligurian Apennines. For long-distance walkers, the *Alta Via dei Monti Liguri* (*see page 11*), which runs the entire length of the Ligurian Apennines, offers a wonderful opportunity to sample the different landscapes of the region. Mountain climbers will find what they're looking for in Pietravecchia, around Albenga and near Finale Ligure.

Further detailed information may be obtained from the Club Alpino Italiano (CAI), Piazza Palermo 11, I-16129 Genoa, tel: 010-310584.

Riding

Horse-riding holidays are growing very popular in Liguria. The hills and mountains inland provide a wide range of opportunities for day trips or treks lasting several days.

For more information, contact the Associazione Nazionale per il Turismo Equestre (ANTE), Vico Campetto 10, I-16123 Genoa, tel: 010-291419.

Sailing

The Ancient Romans and the Ligurians were just as pleased as today's sailors to discover the many excellent mooring locations along the Riviera, and today the marinas and yachting harbours contain all the modern conveniences. Dinghies as well as motorboats are available for hire at the resorts.

More information can be obtained from the Federazione Italiana Vela, Comitato Regionale, Viale Brigato Bisagno 2/17, I-16129 Genoa, tel: 010-589431.

Hiring dinghies is no problem

Surfing

Surfing is possible in almost every resort, and schools and board hire are available in most places. The local tourist information offices can provide more information.

Swimming

The 317-km (196-mile) long coast has no shortage of great places to swim, but only very few of the beaches are freely accessible. This is partly due to the fact that the many hotels own their own beach, and partly because there are no less than 460 *stabilimenti balneari*, or 'bathing areas'. The latter are simply stretches of beach that have been cordoned off and which can only be entered on payment of an admission charge. They can be anything from picturesque bays to long sand or pebble beaches ideal for children. Anyone looking for peace and quiet should head for the rocky part of the coast for a swim; remember, though, that it's not all that easily accessible.

Swim where you can

Winter Sports

Believe it or not, it is possible to ski in Liguria, despite the mild Riviera climate. The region has three winter sports areas, catering for many different kinds of activity: Alberola, near Sassello in the province of Savona, on the northern slope of Monte Beigua (1,287m/4,220ft); Monesi di Triora (province of Imperia), on the Monte Saccarello (2,200m/7,220ft); and last but not least, Santo Stefano d'Aveto (province of Genoa), the best-equipped skiing centre in Liguria.

More information on skiing is available from the Club Alpino Italiano (CAI), Piazza Palermo 11, I-16129 Genoa, tel: 010-310584.

Getting There

Opposite: local transport

By plane

The only international airport in Liguria is Christopher Columbus Airport in Genoa, 7km (4 miles) from the city. British Airways flies twice a day from Gatwick, with a flying time of 1 hour 50 minutes. Contact British Airways Linkline on tel: 0345 222111; in the US 1-800-AIRWAYS. All Alitalia flights involve a change in Rome to join the 5 daily connecting services to Genoa. If not flying via London, American passengers should fly into Rome to make the connection. **Alitalia**: in London tel: 0171 602 7111; New York 212-582 8900; Los Angeles tel: 310-568 0901.

There is a regular bus service called Volabus from Genoa Airport to the city centre which also calls at the two train stations and takes about 30 minutes.

Long-distance connections

By road

There are good motorways all across France, and depending on which route is taken, the passes from France or Switzerland into Italy connect easily to the *autostrada* to Liguria. The Mont Blanc Tunnel and the Great St Bernard Tunnel are among those open year-round. Tolls are charged on Italian motorways.

By bus

There are no direct bus services, but Eurolines operate services from London to Milan where the excellent regional bus services can be used. An alternative would be bus to Milan and then a 2-hour train ride.

By rail

Liguria is served by international main-line services from Nice, Mont Cenis, Gotthard, Germany and Austria. If travelling direct from the UK, take the Eurostar to Gard du Nord in Paris, then cross to Gare du Lyon for the overnight 21.14 to Genoa. Call the Rail Shop on tel: 0990-300003. Many trains travel on from Genoa to Ventimiglia in the west or La Spezia in the east.

Genoa railway station

By boat

The port of Genoa is the most important Mediterranean port of call for both passengers and cargo. It is a destination point from ports of Europe, America, Africa and the other continents. It is served by Mediterranean ferry services (from Sardinia, Sicily and Corsica), and there are regular sailings along the coast to La Spezia, Savona and Imperia. In recent years, cruise holidays have become increasingly popular and thanks to the modern facilities there has been great development in cruising holidays departing from the port of Genoa.

Ferry arrival

Getting Around

Motorists

A national driving licence and country stickers suffice, though a green insurance card is recommended. Breakdown service is usually free of charge for members of automobile clubs. Seat-belts are compulsory in Italy. Never leave anything in the car which might attract thieves – not even for a few moments. Also, remember that the fines for traffic offences in Italy (parking, overtaking, speed limits, etc) are very high.

The following speed limits apply to motor traffic in Italy unless otherwise indicated: 50kmph (30mph) in built-up areas, 90kmph (55mph) on country roads, and 130kmph (75mph) on motorways (*autostrada*). Speed limits are often lowered at weekends or on public holidays. Police checks have become much stricter in recent times, and excessive speed as well as excessive alcohol consumption can cost motorists their licence – this also applies to foreign drivers.

By bus

The buses in Liguria are indispensable for reaching the more remote villages. Major centres have their own local bus services as well as firms operating long-distance and regional routes.

By motorbike

Motorbike fans will really appreciate all the hairpins on the Ligurian roads inland. Motorbike and scooter hire is available in all the main centres.

Easy rider

A local service

By train

One ideal way to avoid all the queues on the coast roads is simply to take the train. Because trains tend to be crowded, however, travellers who haven't booked in advance should arrive at the station at least 30 minutes before departure.

The rail network mirrors that of the motorway network. The main Ventimiglia–La Spezia line serves travellers from Northern Italy arriving from Milan and Turin via Genoa, and connects with the Tyrrenhian Line to and from Rome and Southern Italy. Rapid travel is guaranteed by TEE, EC and IC trains, with conveniently timed connections to all destinations. But there are also slower trains operating along the Ligurian coast, taking in more stops.

There are two stations in Genoa. Principe is the terminal for trains from France, Turin, Milan and Rome. Brignole serves the local lines. The Italian State Railways offer a variety of fare reductions. For information on these and departure times enquire at the local railway stations.

Facts for the Visitor

Sights are well displayed

Travel documents

Visitors from European Union countries require either a passport or identification card to enter Italy. Holders of passports from most other countries do not usually require visas for a period not exceeding three months.

Customs

There have been practically no customs limits for nationals of EU member states since 1993. The following are just rough guidelines: 800 cigarettes, 200 cigars, 1kg of tobacco, 90 litres of wine.

Currency regulations

Unlimited amounts of foreign currency and Italian lire may be brought in and out of Italy, but need to be declared if the sum exceeds L20 million.

Tourist information

Here are the addresses of the Italian Tourist Office (ENIT):
UK: 1 Princes Street, London W1, tel: 0171-408 1254.
US: 630 Fifth Avenue, Suite 1565, New York NY 10111, tel: (212) 245-4822.

When in Liguria, contact the SRPT (Servizio Regionale di Promozione Turistica, Via Fieschi 15, I-16121 Genoa, tel: 010-548 4818, fax: 010-541 046.

Currency and exchange

The unit of currency in Italy is the lira (abbreviated to Lit. or L), which comes in 5, 10, 20, 50, 100, 200 and 500 lire coins, and 1,000, 2,000, 5,000, 10,000, 50,000 and 100,000 lire notes. Foreign and Italian currency not exceeding 20 million lire in value may be brought in and out of the country; larger sums need to be declared.

Eurocheques can be cashed up to a maximum value of 300,000 lire at banks with the EC symbol. Most credit cards, including Visa, Access and American Express, are accepted in hotels, restaurants and shops and for air and train tickets and cash at any bank. All the larger towns in Liguria have automatic bank tellers ('Bancomat').

Tipping
This is expected, despite all-inclusive prices (approximately 10 percent).

Bills and receipts
Not only the Italians themselves but also foreign tourists are expected to have receipts (*ricevuta fiscale*) made out by restaurants, hotels, car repair workshops, etc, listing services rendered plus the correct amount of Italian VAT (IVA) and to keep them on their person for possible checks by the Italian fiscal authorities.

Opening times
Generally, shops are open on weekdays from 9am–7.30pm with a lunch break from 1–3.30pm. Many shops are closed on Saturday and Monday afternoons.

Banks: Monday to Friday 8.30am–1.30pm; some also open in the afternoon from 2.45pm–3.45pm. Money can be exchanged at weekends in the railway stations and airports of the larger cities.

Museum opening hours vary considerably, and the times stated in this book are subject to change. State-owned museums are generally open daily from 9am–2pm, and 9am–1pm on Sunday and public holidays. They are often closed on Monday. Note: some state-owned and municipal museums allow free admission to visitors under 18 and over 60 years of age.

Churches are usually closed around lunchtime, roughly from noon–4pm.

Filling Stations, apart from those on the motorways, are closed at lunchtime and on Sunday and public holidays. Some have cash-operated automatic pumps.

Public holidays
1 January, 6 January (Epiphany), Easter Sunday, Easter Monday, 25 April (National Day of Liberation), 1 May, Whit Sunday, 15 August (Assumption of the Virgin, ferragosto), 1 November, 8 December (Immaculate Conception), and 25 and 26 December (Christmas).

Postal services
Main post offices in major towns are open all day, otherwise the hours are 8am to 1.30pm. Stamps are sold at post offices and tobacconists.

General store

Main post offices are open all day

Telephone

Calls can be made from phone centres run by the phone company TELECOM (not in post offices) or from public phones either using L100, L200 and L500 coins or prepaid phone cards (scheda telefonica) available for L5,000, L10,000 and L15,000 from many newsagents, tobacconists or from TELECOM offices.

There is direct dialling to most countries. Dialling codes from Italy: Australia 0061; United Kingdom 0044; US and Canada 001.

If calling within Italy, note that the area or city codes are now dialled as part of the number even when calling within the same city or area. Thus a Genoa number always has the code 010 attached no matter where you're calling from. And if calling you're calling from abroad, the '0' is always retained.

AT&T: 172-1011, Sprint: 172-1877, MCI: 1721022.

Keeping time

Time

Italy is six hours ahead of US Eastern Standard Time and one hour ahead of Greenwich Mean Time.

Voltage

Usually 220v; occasionally 110v. There are different plugs and sockets for each.

Theft

To prevent theft, don't invite it in the first place: don't leave any valuables inside your car, always lock the vehicle when you leave it, and leave your cash in the hotel safe. When out walking in big towns and cities keep a close eye on your cameras and handbags (especially in the harbour section of Genoa).

Medical

With Form E111 from the Department of Health and Social Security, UK visitors are entitled to reciprocal medical treatment in Italy. There are similar arrangements for other members of EU countries. It may nevertheless be advisable to take out insurance for private treatment in case of accident.

Holiday insurance policies and private patients schemes are recommended for non-EU visitors.

In case of minor ailments, chemists (Farmacia) are well stocked with medicines, often sold without prescription.

Emergencies

Emergency Assistance (Ambulance, fire, police), tel: 113.
Police Immediate Action, tel: 112.
Breakdown service, tel: 116.
Emergency medical assistance, tel: 118.

Firefighters to the rescue

Grandeur in San Remo

A more modest facade

Accommodation

Hotels

With its 2,500 hotels and 180 campsites, the Italian Riviera provides accommodation whatever your budget and your tastes. The hotels (*hotel* or *albergo*) are mostly located at the resorts, and range from one (simple) to five (luxury) stars for comfort and service. Boarding houses *(pensione)* are also plentiful, as are bed and breakfast establishments *(garni)*. For holidays in July and August, however, remember to book any accommodation well in advance; rooms during peak season are usually only available on half or full board. Breakfast is not always included in the price of the room. In winter, many hotels in the coastal resorts are closed, while simpler establishments further inland are almost always open all year round. Brochures listing hotels in Liguria are available from Servizio Regionale di Promozione Turistica, Via Fieschi 15, I-16121 Genoa, tel: 010-548 4918, and from regional information offices.

Camping

Since Liguria is well-equipped with campsites of all categories (1–4 stars), camping fans are spoiled for choice here – if they stay on the coast, that is. Despite the large selection of sites it's still a good idea to book ahead in peak season, since many places are taken by permanent campers. Almost all the campsites are either in or right next to seaside resorts. Camping in official car parks in mobile homes is forbidden in several of the coastal towns. More information on camping, and also a useful brochure listing all the sites, is available from the Servizio Regionale di Promozione Turistica, Via Fieschi 15, I-16121 Genoa, tel: 010-548 5868.

Agriturismo

This is the Italian word for farm holidays, ideal for those keen on spending time close to nature. Families with children are finding these deals increasingly attractive, and *Agriturismo* is an interesting alternative to the more 'usual' Riviera holiday. Farmers rent out rooms or apartments with varying standards of comfort, some reasonably priced and some expensive. For more information contact Agriturist Regionale, Via Invrea 11/10, I-16129 Genoa.

Youth hostels

There are four of these along the Italian Riviera, but only two are open all year round: the 'Priamar' hostel in Savona and the *Albergo per la Gioventú* in Genoa. The 'Wuillermin' hostel in Finale and the 'Villa dei Franceschini' in Savona are closed from mid-September to mid-March, and the 'Cristoforo Colombo' in Genoa from 22 December to 22 January. For more information, contact the Associazione Italiana Alberghi per la Gioventú (AIG), Comitato Regionale, Salita Salvatore Viale 1/18, I-16128 Genoa, tel: 010-586407.

Hotel selection

Here is a selecton of some of the numerous hotels to be found along the Italian Riviera. $$$ = expensive, $$ = medium-priced and $ = inexpensive.

Alassio
$$Firenze, Corso Dante 35, tel: 0182-643 239, fax: 643 146. Old villa by the sea, modernised and comfortable.

Albisola Capo
$$Park Hotel, Via Alba Docilia 3, tel: 019-482 355. Small – only 11 rooms – but really pleasant.

Bordighera
$$$Cap Ampelio, Via Virgilio 5, tel: 0184-264 333, fax: 264 244. Perfect service, beautiful grounds, located up on a hill. **$$Della Punta**, Via Sant'Amelio 27, tel: 0184-262 555. Panoramically situated and right next to the sea for beach fans.

Camogli
$$$Cenobio dei Dogi, Via Cuneo 34, tel: 0185-7241, fax: 772796. Patrician villa with all the modern conveniences.

Cinque Terre
$$Porto Roca, Monterosso al Mare, Via Corone 1, tel: 0187-817 502, fax: 817 692. Right above the sea, with a superb view. **$$Ca'd'Andrean**, Manarola, Via Discovolo 25, tel: 0187-920 040. Comfortable hotel in an old oil-mill.

Enjoy the countryside

93

Alassio

Manarola

$Due Gemelli, Campi near Riomaggiore, Via Litoranea 1, tel: 0187-920 111. Beautifully situated high above the sea, surrounded by vineyards and chestnut groves.

Finalborgo
$$$Punta Est, Via Aurelia 1, tel: 019-600 611, fax: 600 611. Comfortable 18th-century villa right above the sea.

Genoa
$$$Savoia Majestic, Via Arsenale di Terra 15, tel: 010-261 641, fax: 261 883. Near Porta Principe station, modern comforts in a palatial hotel that has accommodated royalty. **$$$La Pagoda**, Via Capolungo 15, tel: 010-372 6161, fax: 321 218. Elegant establishment in the villa region of Nervi. **$$Milano Terminus**, Via Balbi 34, tel: 010-246 2264, fax: 246 7167. Central and comfortable. **$$Agnello d'Oro**, Via delle Monachette 6, tel: 010-246 2084, fax: 246 2327. Nice location, good service. **$$Capannina**, Via Tito Speri 7, tel: 010-317 131, fax: 362 2692. Quiet and right next to the sea in the picturesque suburb of Boccadasse.

La Spezia
$$Firenze e Continentale, Via Paleocapa 7, tel: 0187-713 210, fax: 714 930. Old building with modern and comfortable interior.

Lavagna
$$Giardini, Via Vinelli 9, tel: 0185-313 951, fax: 323 096. Elegant, close to the cathedral. **$Mare e Monti**, Sant'Andrea di Rovereto, Via Aurelia 86, tel: 0185-318 068, fax: 318 068. Family-run, with view across Gulf of Tigullio.

Noli
$$El Sito, Via La Malfa, tel: 019-748 107, fax: 748 5871. Good view, good service.

Porto Maurizio
$$Croce di Malta, Via Scarincio 148, tel: 0183-667 020, fax: 63 687. Modern hotel right by the sea, with view of the harbour.

Portofino
$$$Piccolo Hotel, tel: 0185-269 015, fax: 269 621. Four-star establishment in a well-tended park and magnificent view of the Gulf from its balconies. **$Eden**, Vico Dritto 18, tel: 0185-269 091, fax: 269 047. Centrally located.

Portovenere
$$Paradiso, Via Garibaldi 24, tel: 0187-790 612, fax: 292 582. Nice atmosphere, magnificently situated.

Rapallo
$$Astoria, Via Gramsci 4, tel: 0185-273 533, fax: 274 093. Art nouveau villa right next to the sea. **$$Minerva**, Corso Colombo 7, tel: 0185-230 388, fax: 67078. Central.

San Remo
$$$Royal, Corso Imperatrice 80, tel: 0184-5391, fax: 61445, the most expensive and luxurious hotel in town.

San Terenzo
$$Byron, Via Biaggini, tel: 0187-967 104, fax: 967 409. Right beside the sea with a great view.

Santa Margherita Ligure
$$$Hotel Imperial Palace, Via Pagana 19, tel: 0185-288 991, fax: 0185-284 223. Elegant, historic hotel. **$$Laurin**, Corso Marconi 3, tel: 0185-289 971, fax: 285 709. Traditional hotel near the harbour. **$Villa Anita**, Via Tigullio 10, tel: 0185-286 543. Pleasant place with a park.

Savona
$$Mare, Via Nizza 89, tel: 019-264 065, fax: 263 277. Modern, elegant, right next to the sea.

Sestri Levante
$$Due Mari, Vico Coro 18, tel: 0185-42695, fax: 42698. Nice old villa.

Triora
$Colomba d'Oro, Corso Italia 66, tel: 0184-94051, fax: 94 089. Friendly and clean, in a former monastery.

Royal Hotel

Hotel Imperial Palace

Index